CONTENTS

PREFACE   v

CHAPTER 1
Beyond the Five Senses: 1
    From Misunderstanding to Mystery

CHAPTER 2
Breaking the Bubble: 47
    From Limitation to Life

CHAPTER 3
The Big Bang – or Roar?:   93
    Where Physics Meets Metaphysics

CHAPTER 4
God's Miniature Gods: 133
    The Human Being as Cosmic Library

APPENDIX 1   187

APPENDIX 2   191

ABOUT THE AUTHOR   199

Of
Mystics &
Mistakes

The journey from
confusion to clarity, from
error to enlightenment, from
self-deception to self-discovery

Sadhguru

Yogi, Mystic and Visionary

JAICO PUBLISHING HOUSE

Ahmedabad Bangalore Bhopal Bhubaneswar Chennai
Delhi Hyderabad Kolkata Lucknow Mumbai

Published by Jaico Publishing House
A-2 Jash Chambers, 7-A Sir Phirozshah Mehta Road
Fort, Mumbai - 400 001
jaicopub@jaicobooks.com
www.jaicobooks.com

To be sold only in India, Bangladesh, Bhutan,
Pakistan, Nepal, Sri Lanka and the Maldives.

OF MYSTICS & MISTAKES
ISBN 978-81-8495-308-4

First Jaico Impression: 2012
Twenty-sixth Jaico Impression: 2018

Printed by
SRG Traders Pvt. Ltd.
B-41, Sector 67,
Noida 201301, U.P.

PREFACE

"There are only two types of people: mystics and mistakes," says Sadhguru, leaving most readers in no doubt of the category to which they belong!

That sounds damning. But mistakes can thankfully be rectified. And that's the hope this book holds out to seekers. It reminds us that each one of us can make the journey – from confusion to clarity, from error to enlightenment, from self-deception to self-discovery – if only we choose.

This book is an invitation to a journey – from a life of mechanical autopilot to a life of freedom and grace. It leads readers from narrowly logical categories to spaces far beyond the frontiers of probability, from the realm of fact to landscapes lunar and mysterious. But even as it charts its course, it does not posit any easy polarities; it is evenhanded in its rejection of the dogmas of both science and religion. Sharp, piercing and unsparing, what it represents is mysticism demystified – stripped of the trappings of facile logic and facile illogic, of rigid rationality and rigid faith.

Above all, this is a book that offers signposts on a journey that can so often be a bewildering one. Sadhguru draws the reader's attention to the many perils of self-delusion on the path. Mysticism, he tells us in the very first chapter, denouncing many long-cherished assumptions, has nothing whatsoever to do with thinking about God, yearning for salvation or even attaining peace. And it is emphatically not an expedition for those with "shopping lists."

It is, instead, a journey for those willing to take risks, for those willing to travel beyond the limited and unreliable matrix of logic and the five senses, for those willing to open their doors and windows and let sunlight in. Does it take an act of conversion? Yes. Conversion to total receptivity. "You can convert this human system into absolute receptivity where you can perceive life in ways that you have never believed possible," he says. But he concedes that receptivity doesn't come easy; it entails putting aside one's ideas, emotions and long-held identifications, with no guaranteed dividends in store. And yet, the spiritual life will settle for nothing less. When dominated by the human intellect, life is a mere circus, says Sadhguru. But when dominated by the human intelligence, it is nothing less than a dance.

That dance entails discernment. Sadhguru draws our attention to certain vital distinctions: between the clarity born of fanaticism and the clarity born of realization, between magic and mysticism, between a spurious spirituality and an authentic mysticism. "You saw God. So what the hell?" he remarks caustically, pointing out that the only index of any genuine spirituality is self-transformation. A spiritual process that doesn't produce joyful and intense human beings, he maintains, is worth nothing.

In the second chapter, he tells us just what it takes to break out of self-created cocoons of individuality, how to generate intensity enough to "break the bubble" of space and time. In a subtle and vital distinction, he emphasizes that mysticism is not for those seeking mastery but for those seeking freedom. And the journey towards that freedom – which he describes tantalisingly as an "intoxication" that is "not insanity" – entails an understanding of how to be intense but not tense, relaxed but not lax. The chapter also includes forays into areas that are more obviously non-logical and mysterious: the question of past life memory; the nature of true bliss; the moon and mysticism; and the master's personal account of how the "bubble" was broken in his own life.

The third section takes us even deeper on this voyage into the unknown, pointing out that both modern science and the yogic science intersect at one vital point: in their acknowledgement of the mystery of existence. Here Sadhguru discusses a range of fascinating subjects: the beginnings of the universe; the true meaning of the term "sacrifice"; the yogic process of *linga*-making (the unique subtle energy form of the Dhyanalinga created by him in Coimbatore, as well as the birth of the linga in the ancient temple of Thanjavur); the yogic alchemy of transforming a man into a god; the birthing of a goddess (in which he discusses the Linga Bhairavi temple that he consecrated in 2010); and the significance of living in a consecrated space.

An exciting culmination to the book is the final chapter which covers a gamut of related themes, probing the mystical dimensions of subjects as diverse as dreams and destiny, karma and memory, imagination and meditation, human conception and birth, the human body, liberation and the limitless possibilities of the human spine.

There's something here for every kind of reader. There is Sadhguru's razor-sharp logic in dealing with fluffy illogicality, and his ability to uncover profound truth in seemingly sterile scientific fact. For those inclined to soar too readily into the empyrean, this book will offer a firm anchor to the terrestrial. For those who prefer to remain earthbound, it is likely to offer moments of unexpected free-fall.

Fasten your seatbelts. Both matter-of-fact and wildly improbable, here's a book that crash-lands when you prepare for altitude, and takes off just when you expect to find the earth beneath your feet.

—Arundhathi Subramaniam

CHAPTER 1

BEYOND THE FIVE SENSES
From Misunderstanding to Mystery

*"One little step existentially is worth more than all
the scriptures that you can read on the planet."*

"Sunlight comes into your house not because you want it. It happens because you open the windows."

Sadhguru: Two cows were grazing on an English meadow. One said, "What's your opinion on the Mad Cow disease?" The other said, "I don't care a hoot about it. Anyway, I'm a helicopter."

If a cow realizes that it is a cow, it becomes a celebrity – a holy cow. It is that simple. It is just a question of realization. In India, we have always called mystics "realized" beings. Realization is not about inventing or discovering something; it is just about realizing who you are. If there is something you do not understand, it is mysterious to you. Someone who seems to know what others do not is called a mystic. But the mystic is just someone who has realized what is there. Others don't because they are too self-engrossed to pay any attention to life.

Mysticism: what exactly do we understand by the word? That which cannot be understood through logic usually gets termed mystical. Or in other words, that which you are unable to comprehend through the five sense organs gets labeled mystical.

Let me give you an example. I am sitting here; suppose you

could not see me, but you heard my voice – that would be very mysterious, wouldn't it? Now you can see me here, but my voice can be heard all over. Do you see that my voice is coming from everywhere? Is this not mysterious? "Oh, this is just a microphone," you say. You have an explanation for it, so it is not mysterious. But anything that you cannot explain logically, all those things are considered mysterious.

Right now the logical dimension of thought is filtering life through the intellect. The logical process has become so dominant simply because right now perception is limited to the five senses. The very nature of sense perception is such that it always perceives everything in bits and pieces. It always divides everything into at least two; it never perceives anything as one. If you can see this part of my hand (*turns his hand, revealing his palm*), you cannot see that part of my hand. If you see this part, you cannot see the other. This is so even if you take a grain of sand; if you perceive one part of it, you do not perceive another.

So the moment you perceive everything through the five sense organs, the world gets divided. And only when there is a division, there is logic. If there is only one, there is no logic; only if there are two, there is logic. So the foundation of the logical mind is in dividing the world. And if you do not divide existence, you cannot employ your logic. So sense perception and logical thinking, or logical understanding, are directly connected; they are complementary to each other.

Now what cannot be contained in logic – or what cannot be perceived by the sense perceptions – is what we are referring to as "mystical." That dimension of truth which cannot be boxed into your logical mind is being labeled "mystical." When you say, "we want to explore mysticism," you are saying that you are willing to go beyond your present levels of understanding and experience, and look for the truth. So our logical mind will not be of use to us here. Only what has been fed to you through the filters of your five sense organs is the content of your logic. And these sense organs are not reliable.

Today neuroscientists are going to great lengths to prove that almost everything that you have known as true until now is false – what you see, hear, smell and taste is not true. It is a big deception. Nothing is the way it seems. This research has been going on in a very serious fashion only for the last few years. In these four-five years, everything that we knew as true has become untrue. Everything that we thought of as illusory has become true. Now neuroscientists are telling you that what you see is not reality. Physicists were telling you this to an extent, but neuroscientists are now confirming it to you. They can prove to you with experimentation that everything that you see around you – the shapes and forms, colors and sizes – none of this is true. I think, way back, Indian mystics told you everything is *maya* (illusion), isn't it? (*Laughs*) When we say something is an illusion, it does not necessarily mean that it does not exist. It simply means you are not seeing it the way it is.

As you know, what is light for you is darkness for somebody else. What is darkness for you is light for somebody else. In the next few hours the sun will set, and you will experience darkness; a whole range of creatures will come awake, because for them darkness is an alarm bell. The day has begun for them. On this planet, there is more life which is nightlife – and I am not talking about Mumbai people! (*Laughs*) I am talking about the creatures that are made that way. In terms of population, they are more than you. These nocturnal creatures outnumber the day creatures by far. So with whom are you going to argue as to which is light and which is darkness? If you and an owl sit together and start an argument as to which is light and which is darkness, where would it take you? Into an endless argument!

Maya is not just on this level. Even the very shapes and sizes that you see are not the way they are. There are many creatures here, right now in the grass. They actually do not see you, because they do not see sizes beyond a certain proportion at all; it is not relevant to their survival. You do not see all the

microbes, do you? In the same manner, they do not see you.
(*Laughs*) You are not important for them.

So our perception through the sense organs is very limited. And
so what we refer to as the mystical is that dimension of life
which we are unable to perceive through our sense organs, or
deduce through our logical process. When our logic fails,
anything that does not look logical becomes mysterious. So
right now because your perception is limited to the five senses,
the mystical can only be a fantastic story that you either believe
or disbelieve. I want you to understand the difference between
the mystical and the magical. "Harry Potter" is selling in
millions today. That's not mysticism; that's magic – and that's
different. When we seek to experience the mystical, we are not
looking for entertainment; we are looking for a solution to our
lives.

When I say "solution," the inevitable question is, do I have a
problem? The answer is yes, because whoever you are, you
want to be a little more than what you are. When that "little
more" happens, you want to be a little more than that. It is a
problem, isn't it? In other words, you are attempting to become
boundless. Now attempting to seek the boundless through the
physical is a serious problem. Seeking that which is boundless
or infinite through your physical nature is just like wanting to
go to the moon on a bullock cart. When this fails, someone tells
you as a solution: "Get yourself a new whip and you will get
there." Believe me, you are not going to get there. You may kill
the bulls, but you will not get there!

See, this human system has come with a different kind of
possibility. As an instrument of perception, if you raise it in
pitch, you will see it can perceive things in a completely
different way from what people normally perceive for the sake
of survival.

This happened in 2009. An ex-president, not knowing what to
do after his retirement (and how long to stay in his Texas
ranch), got invited to Australia. Now because he likes to live in
the open country, they put him up in a large, well-equipped

ranch. The farmer, who was in charge of this ranch, took the ex-president for a walk in the evening. As they were walking, the rancher, trying to offer some information about the place, said, "This is a 1000-acre ranch."

The ex-president said, "Oh, that's nothing! In Texas, no ranch is less 5000 acres."

The rancher became quiet. They walked quietly for some time. He saw one of his prize cows standing there. The rancher very proudly pointed to the cow and said, "This is our prize cow. It yields about seventy-six liters of milk per day."

Without even looking at it, the ex-president dismissed the cow and said, "Ah, that's nothing. Our longhorns in Texas are twice the size and give five times the milk."

After that, the rancher did not say anything; they walked on quietly. As they were walking, suddenly a kangaroo hopped in their way and hopped off. The ex-president looked at this creature incredulously and asked, "What is that?"

So the Australian rancher said, "Why, you guys in Texas, haven't you seen a grasshopper?" (*Laughter*)

So, this tiny little piece of life that we call an insect (tiny, if you consider his size compared to yours), just look at his physical prowess. Whatever the length of his body, he can jump almost fifty to hundred times more than you. Just see, any animal in nature, in terms of physical prowess, is made better than you. Whether it is a worm or an insect or a bird or any animal, they are all made better. You have all this muscle, but just do this (*flaps his arms*) for one hour and see if anything happens! But you have birds flying all the way from Siberia down to South India, some of them almost nonstop. So in terms of physical prowess, you cannot compare yourself to any creature on the planet.

But human beings came with a few different possibilities. We came with a certain capability of doing something beyond our instinct of survival. That is the most important thing: that you can handle life beyond the needs of survival. If you don't, you will only understand eating, sleeping, reproducing and dying one day. That is all life will be. That is all life is for every creature on this planet. Most human beings, instead of looking beyond the needs of survival, have just raised their standards of survival. Survival at one time meant just getting a meal or two meals a day. Now survival means you must have a Mercedes. We are just raising the bar for survival, but it is still just survival. This is an unintelligent way of using this human mechanism. This one creature – the human being – came with a slightly higher possibility. You just have to be willing to explore the full dimension and depth of what this possibility is.

In every part of the world, there have been men and women who raised their sense perception beyond the five senses. Women usually got burnt – that is why there have been mainly men. In most parts of the world if a woman claimed she saw something more than what is there, she was killed. Not in India, but in many other places this has happened. This is the reason why historically, even though there have been many women mystics, they have not been heard of.

There is a beautiful story about Swami Vivekananda[1]. He was the first yogi who went to the West and caused a little stir out there, a little over hundred years ago. He landed up in Chicago, and then he went to Europe.

When he was in Germany, he was the guest of a well-known poet and philosopher of that time. After dinner, they met in the study where they sat conversing. There was a book on the table which was partially read by this person and because the man was talking very highly about the book, Swami Vivekananda said, "Give it to me for an hour; let me see what's there in the book." That man felt a little insulted and said, "What, for an hour? What will you know in an hour? I've been reading this for weeks and I'm not getting anywhere. And above all, it's in the German language. You don't know the German language;

---

1 The best known of the disciples of Ramakrishna Paramahamsa, Vivekananda is often considered as a role model for Indian youth.

how will you read it?" Vivekananda said, "Give it to me for an hour; let me see." Just as a joke it was given to him.

He took the book, placed it between his two hands and just sat there for an hour, then gave back the book and said, "There is nothing worthwhile in this book." That man thought, "This is real arrogance. He doesn't even open the book. It's in a language that he doesn't know, and he makes a judgment about the whole book!" He said, "This is nonsense." Vivekananda replied, "You ask me anything about the book. Which page do you want, tell me." So suppose he said "page six hundred and seventy-three," Vivekananda just repeated that page verbatim. He never opened the book. He just held it between his hands. But he could just repeat any page. That man could not believe this. He said, "What is this? How can you do this without opening the book and in a language that you don't know?" So Vivekananda said, "That's why I'm Vivekananda." "*Viveka*" means perception. His real name was Naren. His guru named him "Vivekananda" because he embodied such remarkable perception.

Now, this world has seen many beings with heightened levels of perception, but the one that we can call "Ultimate Perception" is Shiva himself. When we say "Shiva," do not look at him according to his popular depiction. In the yogic traditions, Shiva is not seen as God. He is seen as the Adiyogi, or the first yogi, and the Adi Guru, the first guru. One of the most significant aspects of Shiva is the fact that he has a third eye. This does not mean that he is some kind of a freak with his forehead cracked open! It means that his perception has gone beyond the five sense perceptions. What these two eyes cannot see, he is able to see.

As I said before, whatever you see with these two eyes is a mistake. Only when you see beyond that do you become a mystic. So there are only two kinds of people: mystics and mistakes. There is a big mistake about the way we are perceiving life. When it gets corrected, people think you are a mystic because you are beginning to perceive life in such a way that you can never fit into logic. Logic is just a small part of your life. You can fit logic into your life but never life into logic. So once you know that you are a mistake, then you are a potential mystic.

Just look at the nature of your existence right now. You know a lot about the world, but you do not know anything about yourself. This is a ridiculous way to live, isn't it? One who does not know himself, can he know the world? When you are unable to grasp what is within, do you really believe you can grasp everything outside?

When it comes to outside realities, all of us are differently capable. No two human beings are equally capable when it comes to doing something on the outside. But when it comes to your interiority, all of us are equally capable. There is no question of incapability. It is just a question of willingness. Are we willing? That is the question.

You can convert this human system into absolute receptivity, where you can perceive life in ways that you have never believed possible. If you keep all your ideas, emotions and your nonsense aside, maybe you can take a step, move one inch. One little step existentially is worth more than all the scriptures that you can read on the planet. One little step is far more important than all the philosophies that you can spout.

Now, if you had a choice, why would anybody be a mistake? Nobody wants to be one. The reason you are a mistake is just because you start shopping for things too early.

Once Shankaran Pillai was arrested for theft just before Diwali and was brought to the court. The judge was ready for Diwali, and he was in a festive mood. He was feeling a little compassionate, and he said to Shankaran Pillai, "Why did you get yourself into trouble, just before Diwali? What is the problem?"

Shankaran Pillai said, "Oh my lord, I just went out shopping a little too early, that's all."

The judge said, "That's not a crime. That is very judicious. That's thinking ahead. Nothing wrong with shopping early. When did you start shopping?"

Shankaran Pillai said, "I went shopping before the shops opened." (*Laughter*)

So you start shopping a little too early. That is the only problem! Before your doors are open, you started doing spirituality. You started talking God, heaven, *nirvana*, everything. Now don't talk God, nirvana, *mukti*[2], mysticism; just learn to open your eyes to everything. Perception happens not because you want it. Sunlight comes into your house not because you want it. It happens because you open the windows. You don't have to send an invitation to the sun: "Please enter our house." You open the window and it floods in. So all you have to do is open up your perception. Don't go in search of God. Don't go in search of freedom. You just open your doors and windows. What has to happen will happen. It is not for you to decide what should happen. But if you go shopping too early, and you already have a shopping list, you will forget to open the doors. That is why your whole life is spent talking about it, thinking about it and reading about it. Mysticism will not happen because you have thought about it; it will not happen because you have read about it; and it will not happen because you have heard a lot about it. This "thinking spirituality," "talking spirituality," "reading spirituality," has gone on too much and too long.

Once it happened: a ninety-three year-old man went to his doctor for a medical checkup. The doctor was checking his blood pressure, his heart, and other medical parameters. But the old man squeaked, "Doctor, this is not what I want you to check. I am really worried about my sex life." The doctor asked, "Oh, your sex life, which part of it? Thinking about it or talking about it?"

---

2 Nirvana or mukti: release, liberation, final absolution of the self from the chain of death and rebirth. The highest goal of all spiritual seekers.

Once I told someone, "It is very easy to transcend. If you just keep yourself aside, you will transcend in a moment." They said, "That is easier said than done." I said, "No, it is more difficult to say it than to do it." (*Laughs*) How to speak of an illogical dimension within the framework of logical language? It is more difficult to say it than to do it. It does not matter how many words I use, language will not make you experience the mystical. But at least it will demolish all the wrong things that you have concluded about mysticism. We are still hoping that when everything that you thought to be the truth collapses, you will step into another dimension. But if you really manage to keep yourself aside, then it is very easy. In one moment it can be done.

A while ago, when I was taking a large group of people on a Himalayan trek, one American lady asked me a question. She asked, "Sadhguru, for the last four-and-a-half years I have been with you, and it has been so wonderful to have you as a guru. How does it feel for you to have us as your disciples?" (*Laughs*) I said, "See, being a yogi is fantastic; I would not be any other way. But being a guru is frustrating, because what can be done in a moment, people make you wait for a lifetime to do it."

It could be just done in a moment. If everybody who came here, came absolutely willing, it would be just a moment's job.

 "If your heart stops beating, you would call it an emergency. Then why do you want your mind to stop?"

Questioner: Sadhguru, you say that if we are willing to transcend, it takes only a moment. I don't understand. What does this willingness mean? Must I do nothing and just be myself, in a given moment? Is there something specific I must or must not do?

Sadhguru: See, right now you are a helpless process of thought and emotion. Thought and emotion is not something that you decide. They are just happening all the time, isn't it? And what is the nature of your thought? What is the nature of your emotion? Let's look at this.

Once it happened: two Irishmen were working on a street outside a London brothel. They found, as they were working, that a Protestant priest came near the brothel, looked this way, that way, rolled up his collar, put his head down and ducked into the brothel. They looked at each other and said, "What else can you expect out of a Protestant priest? A Protestant and a prostitute – not much difference. What else can you expect?"

They continued their work. After some time a Jewish rabbi came, looked around, rolled up his collar real high, put his head down, put the umbrella over his head and walked into the brothel. Then both of them looked at each other in distress. "What has happened to the world? A holy man! Just look at him going into the brothel." They were pained.

Then a bishop came down the road, looked this way and that, put his cloak on and went into the brothel. So one of the men said, "One of the girls must be really ill." (*Laughter*)

It all depends what you are identified with, isn't it? Because your mind always works around an identification. Once you are identified with something, you cannot help it. If you think you are an Indian or a Hindu, or a Christian, or a Muslim, immediately your thought process starts working around that. Your emotions are around that to such an extent that whatever you are identified with, you are even willing to die for it, isn't it? It is considered a great thing.

See, the whole idea of a nation is just about 150 to 200 years old. Before that most people on this planet did not belong to any nation. But today, see how we are identified. Especially here in India, not so long ago, this whole country was many kingdoms. But then somebody floated the idea of one nation, and within a few decades it became one nation. We all started thinking that this is India, and India should become free. Before the English came, there was no India. They came and they made it into one nation. And then we picked up on that idea and we said, "This is India."

For some disastrous reasons, it got split up into three pieces. Now you see, on this side of the Line of Control you breathe one way; on the other side of the Line of Control you breathe another way! Cross that Line and see how it feels. I have seen people who stayed there for too long; the moment they cross the border they fall down and kiss the earth. You could have kissed the earth on the other side also. Wherever you kiss it, you only get mud in your mouth. (*Laughs*) You don't get anything else, do you? But just because you are identified – because you feel "this is my country" – just see how the mud tastes good on this side and bitter on that side!

Now this is okay for national or social purposes. But when you are talking about a spiritual dimension, the moment you get identified, you have already lost the possibility of perception. The moment you are identified with something that you are not, you are an endless thought, a compulsive thought; you cannot help it. That is the reason why your thought process is going on endlessly, continuously. Many people are struggling to either stop their thought process or control their thought process. But you do what you want, you cannot control it. It is like you have eaten bad fruit, and now your stomach is full of gas – you cannot stop it; it happens in the most inappropriate moments!

This is happening in the most inappropriate moments as well: you want to meditate and you know what happens. (*Laughter*) You want to pray, you want to think about God, but all kind of nonsense is going on in your head, isn't it? You want to look at somebody and be in love with them, but you look at them, and so many other things are happening. (*Laughs*) Because the moment you are identified with something that you are not, your mind is a compulsive thought process. You cannot help it. It is immaterial what kind of thought is running through your head. Whatever stuff you have inside, your mind runs that, because thought is compulsive.

So how can you perceive something with all these noises happening? Suppose you want to enjoy some music, the first thing is you look for some quiet space, isn't it? If you want to perceive something the way it is, these noises, these endless thoughts, must stop. But if you try to stop them, they will never stop. This is like a car where all the three pedals are accelerators. Whichever you touch, it only goes! There are no brakes in your mind. However you try to stop it, it only goes faster and faster, because once you are identified with something, from that identity whatever you do, you only multiply the thought process. You cannot reduce it.

One moment, suppose you are just looking at the sunset, you forget about yourself. Who you are, whether you are a man or a woman, your qualification, your nation, your religion, everything – you forget that just by looking at the sunset. There is a moment of quiet. Then you think, "If I look at the sunset, I will become quiet." But try it every day. Along with the sunset, all the nonsense in your mind will also go on. One day you go to the mountains, and suddenly because of the immensity of the mountains, you become quiet. Go and live there and see. The same nonsense will happen there. Everything that happens in Mumbai will happen in the mountains. Do not have any doubts about that. Maybe the outside noises will cease, but the inside noises will not cease.

So all it takes is to just sit here as a piece of life. Not as a man or a woman, not as a Hindu or a Muslim, not as anything, but just as a piece of life. That is all you are. Right now, you are so strongly identified with your physical body. What you call "my body" right now, is just a little piece of earth, isn't it? It pops up from the earth, prances around, falls back, becomes a part of it again; a very simple process.

Just look at the long-term span of this creation; you are just a tiny happening. You think too much of yourself – that is the problem. You are so full of yourself that nothing can happen except little things. So if you want something big to happen to you – if you want something beyond what has happened to you until now to touch your life – do not think so much of yourself. "No," you say, "I am very humble; I am the humblest man on this earth." See, again you must be number one! (*Laughter*) Whichever way, you must be number one. If you become important in the world, it is good. But within yourself, do not become so important, because that is a sure way to get lost.

How to become unimportant? This is a simple method: just look carefully at every thought that arises in your mind. Other people may be impressed with what you have said because of how you deliver your ideas, but your thoughts are quite stupid, aren't they? They are just going on with the same nonsense forever. Just see that "all my thoughts are stupid." And emotions are just the juicier part of the thought; so "if my thoughts are stupid, my emotions are even more stupid." You have become important only because you believe what you think and feel is very important. Just make them unimportant. Then suddenly if you sit here, you will simply sit, without any nonsense going on within you.

One of the reasons to put you through these horrible discourses is just that. (*Laughs*) So you go on listening to somebody who overwhelms you with another kind of logic. Then you simply realize: "Oh! I didn't see this before." But your system knows all these things already. Maybe your mind does not know these things, but your system does. Whatever my system knows, your system knows also. You think it doesn't, but it does. Maybe you are not able to articulate that, because you have not paid attention to it. That's all. Otherwise whatever is there in this (*pointing to himself*), is there in everybody. If you keep your thought process aside, or reduce it, then you will see slowly the other dimensions of life become more and more prominent in you.

Right now you are a psychological process and a social process. You are not an existential process. When you say "myself," you are not talking about the life that you are. You are talking about a bundle of thoughts, emotions, ideas, opinions, philosophies, and ideologies maybe, but that's all. Essentially, thought and emotion. If you make these two things unimportant, there is room for something to happen. Life is very, very simple and direct, but the mind is very complex and devious. If you do not pay any attention to it, it will settle down.

Another reason why the mind is going on endlessly – especially when you try to meditate, it takes on a new pitch altogether – is because you have a prejudice against it. You believe, "When I am meditating, no thoughts should come. Even when I am sitting here, I am thinking of something else. What do I do?" It is okay. Whatever your mind is thinking right now – whether you are thinking of Mumbai or mangoes – it does not matter. Just be here like you would sit in a cinema. Simply be with me. Do not worry about what your body and mind are doing.

Why are you so prejudiced against the mind? Do you ever put such conditions upon the body? Do you ever think, "Oh, I am in a spiritual discourse, so my heart should not beat, my blood should not flow." (*Laughs*) If your heart stops beating, you would call it an emergency. Then why do you want your mind to stop? Only because you are paying too much attention to it. You are not paying attention to your heart beating, so it is not a distraction. Isn't your body performing more complex functions than your mind right now? If you pay attention to all that, can you pay attention to what I am saying? No. So you have learned to ignore that. Similarly, it does not matter what the mind is doing once you identify it as a fool. If there is somebody very stupid around you who goes on blabbering, do you not learn to simply ignore him and carry on with your work? That is all you need to do.

Many of you are married, aren't you? You know how to ignore the other person and carry on with your work, don't you? If you did not know, you would not be married this long. (*Laughter*) If you paid attention to every word that was said, and if you reacted to all that, you would not live together. You have learned to pay attention to some things and ignore a lot of other things. So it is okay to treat your mind just like that. Just treat it like a long-time husband. (*Laughs*) He is saying so many things, but it is okay. Some days he comes home drunk; some days he is upset; some days he is something else. It's all right. What he says does not matter. You love him; that is all that matters, isn't it?

Treat your mind like that and you will become very receptive. Don't try to stop it. Don't try to fight it, because you cannot fight it. You have no means to fight it. The fight is just a joke because you are fighting your mind with your mind. It is a trickster. If you try to play any game with it, it will trick you. "It's okay, you play your game," you can tell your mind, "but I am not going to play the game with you." Then your mind will slowly recede. Even if it is not receding, there is no problem. Once it does not bother you, even if it plays its own game, you just let it be. If you do this, your receptivity will rise.

After all, every human being is capable of knowing. Nobody has come impaired in any way. It is just that life never forces itself upon you. This is the way of life. Divinity never forces itself upon you. If you are willing, it is always there for you. If you are not willing, it is not there for you. So all you need to do is create the right kind of willingness and receptivity. Just to bow down and not have a will of your own is the biggest receptivity. It is the easiest way to receive.

If you demolish all your limited assumptions and you sit here blank, that is when you are receptive. Then there is a blast of energy, which is true knowing. See, in my experience, knowledge and energy are not two different things. When you receive a certain energy, you also get to know something.

So essentially, when you sit with me, you receive just a blast of energy. This is how the transmission of mysticism happens. I have said this before: when it comes to the mystical dimensions of life, if I can share even two percent of what I really know, I would consider myself very fortunate. The rest will go away. Or maybe I have been fortunate enough to invest it in the form of the Dhyanalinga[3]. For those who are willing, it will always open up the doors. But with actual live people, if I can share even two percent, that is great. Many mystics could not find a way to give expression to even two percent of what they know.

 "If you want God as a tranquilizer, it is okay as an idea, but if you want the Divine to be an awakening process in your life, an idea is not good enough."

Questioner: When I heard one of your CDs at a friend's place, I was completely disillusioned. (*Sadhguru laughs*). I didn't want to hear a word of what you were saying. But why is it that your presence today makes me listen to you? Is it your physical presence that is making a difference or is it because my senses are in better shape today? (*Laughter*) And most importantly, are you against the idea of God?

Sadhguru: (*Laughs*) You said, "the idea of God." Why would I be against any idea of yours? What does it matter what your idea is? You can have any idea you want. You can have ideas about God, you can have ideas about devil. (But don't have ideas about me! They are bound to be wrong!) (*Laughter*) With God also maybe they are wrong, but he can't protest. I can. (*Laughs*)

Our ideas about God, whatever they are, are essentially ours, isn't it? So if, as you admit, it is only an idea, then there is no problem. But if you are trying to make it into an ideology and spread it, that is a problem, isn't it?

See, that is the beauty of the Indian culture: the fact that everybody can have their own idea of God. If I love this flower,

3 A powerful energy form consecrated by Sadhguru exclusively for the purpose of meditation at Isha Yoga Center.

I can worship it. Nobody thinks it is funny in this country. If there is a stone in my garden and I start worshipping it tomorrow, my neighbors won't think it is funny. They will just think, "He is worshipping a rock-god," you know. If I worship a tree in my garden, nobody will think it is funny. It is a tree-god, that's all! If I worship my mother or my wife or my daughter, nobody will think it is absurd. They will think it is fine. That is beautiful. But if I insist my wife is god for you also, now there is a problem! (*Laughter*)

So your idea of god is not the problem. You want to make an ideology of your idea: that is a serious problem. In this country we have thirty-three million gods and goddesses. And this thirty-three million happened when our population was thirty-three million. Since then we lost our imagination. We became too English in our minds, and we stopped creating gods. And that is creating problems. If each one of us had our own god, we could never organize a group and fight with somebody. Only because a hundred people have gathered behind one god, there is an issue, isn't it? You cannot deny the power and the destructive nature of that ideology. All of us have suffered in some way or the other from this. Humanity has suffered immensely from ideologies of God, isn't it?

And, first of all, where does this need for an idea come? See, there are two ways of approaching something. Let us say, you don't know anything about me. One way is to make an association, to get to know me. Another one way is, sit there and make your own idea about me. Which do you think is closer to reality? If you are interested in truth, you must explore me, isn't it? If you make your own idea about me, that is your idea; it has nothing to do with me.

So when you talk of "ideas," why are you so compulsive about forming ideas about God? Why don't you see that the idea about God has simply come because most human beings are not sincere or straight enough to even admit to themselves they don't know anything about this existence. You do not understand just anything about the nature of this existence. So you want one childish explanation about somebody sitting up there, and how everything is going to be fine, and how he is going to take care of me. This is just coming from a childish idea of insecurity. This is not a search for truth.

On the other hand, "I do not know" is a tremendous possibility. You are trying to destroy that tremendous possibility with your idea. Why don't you live with "I do not know?" If you live with "I do not know," the longing to know will come. If the longing to know comes, the seeking to know will come; if the seeking comes, you will try to find a way to know. Instead of trying to find a way to know, you are just coming up with your own idea which is comfortable and helps you sleep well tonight. If you want God as a tranquilizer, it is okay as an idea, but if you want the Divine to be an awakening process in your life, an idea is not good enough. You need to access that process, isn't it?

So it is only because you are unable to explain the basis of this creation that you invent a Creator. Because you are human, mostly you come up with a human form. If you had some other form, obviously you would have come up with that kind of form. I am sure earthworms are thinking that God is the longest earthworm in the existence, isn't it?

So all your ideas are springing from what you are exposed to. Those are very limited ideas obviously. Because you are Indian, you have certain idea of God. If you were born somewhere else, you would have another idea of God. These are just ideas which are culturally nurtured. Now, in this culture, we did not fix one form to God. Anybody can invent whatever kind of God he wants. There is something called "*ishta devata.*" This means you can make up a god of your choice. No other culture has given you this freedom. That is fantastic, you know. If you don't like any of the thirty-three million choices you have, you can go home and create your own new god today and worship it, and nobody thinks it is funny or absurd! So that is wonderful, because you understand that God is of your making. If you understand God is of your making, there is no

problem, but if you think everybody is of God's making, then
there is a serious problem.

Questioner: But as a mystic, what is *your* idea?

Sadhguru: And suppose I don't have any idea? See, our ideas of
God have come to us only because we tasted creation. We
wanted an explanation for creation, so we created a Creator in
our minds. Does he exist or not? I am not questioning that. I
am just talking about your experience. Right now, the only
thing that you have is belief. And I want you to understand, the
conflict in the world today is not between good and evil, as
people are projecting it to be. The conflict is always between
one man's belief and another man's belief. You believe in one
thing; somebody else believes something else; immediately there
is conflict. Now, what you believe or disbelieve has nothing to
do with reality. It has simply got to do with how much
influence somebody has had upon you.

See, if a god is sitting up in heaven, we don't know how to get
there. Though people have been promising us that they will
take us there for a long time, you did not see anybody who
went there and came back and tell you, "Yes, this is it!" They
have been promising us for a long time – in every culture – that
they are going to take us to heaven. They promise heaven
because they are making a hell out of this place. (*Laughs*)

Now the only thing that you have in your experience is what is
called "you." You can experience this being. When you were
born, you were only so much in size; now you have become this
big. Something within you is creating you, isn't it? Or in other
words, the source of creation seems to be functioning from
right within you. So if you really want to know reality, you
must see how to turn your attention inward. There is a simple
way to do this and begin to experience how this source of
creation is functioning from within you. If this experience

comes into the grasp of a human being, then everything about him will change.

 "Mysticism is like pure science; it has no use. Mysticism is just the human longing to know... Occult is not science. Occult is just technology."

Questioner: In most people's perception, spirituality is synonymous with certain paranormal powers. What is the difference between mysticism and occult?

Sadhguru: One big problem is that mysticism and occult have always been mistaken to be the same. In the US, for example, there has never been any mysticism. But always people thought Native Americans were mystical. No. They have been occult practitioners. You have heard of Native American shamans becoming wolves, becoming eagles, being in two different places at the same time. All this is occult. Actually we have a much more sophisticated form of occult in India, particularly in South India. So if you come with cancer, it could just be gone in ten minutes; but this is not mysticism or spirituality; this is occult. Or I could appear in two different places; this is occult, not mysticism.

Occult was very meaningful when there was no modern technology. Right now, instead of using my cell phone to ask you to come here from wherever you are, suppose I spoke to you directly, that would be occult. But now if I speak to you through occult, you may know it happened, but if you tell people around you, they will all laugh at you. If nobody confirms what you heard, you will start doubting it yourself. Even though it was one hundred percent clear to you, ten people have to confirm it. If they don't confirm, you do not have a stable enough situation in your mind to believe it. But if I call you using a phone, even if you doubt it, there is a "missed call" to prove it! You have evidence.

As modern technology develops, suppose I want to send peanuts to you, I would send it by FedEx or DHL or some other courier. That is one way. Now, without using DHL, if I make a peanut land in your house, this is occult, and this is very much possible. I can have this peanut land in your hand, just like that. This is occult, but this is becoming more and more irrelevant as modern technology develops.

In the past, if you were my ardent disciple who lived in Delhi, and I was in Coimbatore, if I wanted to give you an instruction, it was impractical for me to walk all the way to Delhi. So I spent my time mastering occult so I could deliver this instruction to you. But now that I have a cell phone, why should I? I can still do it, but to prepare you to be receptive enough, to be clear enough to receive it and not doubt it, will take an unnecessarily long time. So I would rather give you my number!

So occult is becoming irrelevant because modern technology is developing into various areas. But mysticism is not something that you can use. Mysticism is like pure science; it has no use. It is just the human longing to know. So getting forces to rally behind mysticism is a tough thing. If I tell you, "You come to Kailash[4], your disease will vanish," I will have ten thousand people traveling with me. (Laughs) But if I tell you, "You come there, and you will know something," only a hundred people will travel with me. Even in that hundred, ninety will be just curiosity seekers; maybe there will be ten really wanting to know. But with occult they will gather very easily.

In Delhi, who are the most popular people? Fortune-tellers. Everybody is lining up behind them, isn't it? Now this kind of fortune-telling is just about your ability to use the mind. Every human being can do this, if his head is not full of all kinds of ideas. The more ideas he has, the less he can use his mind, because ideas are hurdles, ideas are your creation. If you just

---

4   A sacred mountain peak located in Tibet, considered to be the abode of Shiva. Every year, Isha Foundation arranges a pilgrimage to this powerful space.

perceive reality as it is, if you perceive people around you as they are, then the mind is just a continuous flow.

So if you raise this thought process to a certain pitch, if you can back this up with your energy, then this becomes occult. Now let's say I have an intention: I want this peanut to land in your hands in Delhi. If I can back this up with my energy, this will land there. If you focus your mind on something and you are also able to channelize a little bit of your energy behind it, it is bound to happen. That is, if your energies are fluid enough. Or it may be done using a certain ritual or process to get yourself into the state. So backing up your mind with energy is occult. This is a simplistic explanation for the occult sciences.

Occult is not spirituality. Occult is just technology. It is like being able to talk to somebody in Delhi or the United States without the cell phone. Now, from Graham Bell's instrument, it has come to this cell phone. A day will come when this cell phone is not necessary either. Already, I have a Bluetooth mechanism where I don't have to dial. If I just say the person's name, it dials for me. If I say, "Ashram," it will go to the ashram number. A day will come where even this will not be needed. A small implant here (*points to the head*) will be enough. Whomever I want to talk to anywhere in the world, it will just happen.

So occult means that without the blue chip you still manage to talk. It is just physical technology on a different level, that's all. I hesitate to use the word, "subjective," but it is still subjective because you are not using any external objects. You are just using your body and mind and energy to do these things. Initially, if you wanted to manufacture a phone or an instrument you had to take a considerable amount of external material. Now you are only taking a little external material, and trying to reduce that further and further. So a day will come when we don't need any external material; that will be occult. Modern science and occult are bound to meet somewhere.

So empowering your thought can produce certain results for now. You can improve your career, you can improve your income, you can improve your relationships. But all these are extremely superficial aspects of your life. You have a good relationship with your husband or wife or your child; this looks like everything to you right now. But it is a superficial aspect of your life. Right now your job is going well. But it is an extremely superficial aspect of your life. You are making good money. Yes, it creates a certain comfort and well-being for you, I understand. But still, it is very superficial. Most of the time, thought is only playing on this level. It is never addressing the deeper dimensions of who you are. I am not even talking about the being, I am talking about the mind, about the personality. Even the person that you are, it is never touching the deeper dimensions of the person.

So, if your thought and emotion is kept in a certain way, then slowly your energies will join; now this becomes a powerful tool. But it is on a surface level. It will create the right kind of ambience, but it will never fix the problem as such; it cannot. It can open up the door, but it is not the real thing. Occult could be used as a stepping stone to a spiritual process, because in many ways it is the final step of physicality. The subtlest point of physicality is what we are using in occult. If you take information technology, what started as a stone tablet has now come to a tiny blue chip. What would take a whole mountain to be carved upon, today is encoded in a tiny chip. So the physical has become subtler and subtler. Occult is using the subtlest phenomenon of the physical. Because it is the last step in physicality, it can also be used as a stepping stone to go beyond the physical. So in that sense it is significant, but by itself it is not.

 "Intelligence beyond logic is what you are referring to as God."

Questioner: If to perceive the mystical one has to drop the logical, how does a *gnana yogi* – a seeker on the path of knowledge – progress on the path? Isn't that path all about using the logical mind and dissecting things?

Sadhguru: Now a gnana yogi means someone who uses his intellect to start with and then moves on to using his intelligence. The logical intellect cannot approach dimensions of the beyond because it is unable to grasp it. That is why we are referring to the beyond as "mystical." Only because your intellect is unable to grasp it, you are labeling it "mystical."

So how would a man of intellect approach it? A gnana yogi – if he is truly a gnana yogi and not just a bombastic intellectual – understands that the logical intellect can never function without information. If there is no information, logic cannot function. You understand what I am saying? The logical intellect is purely information technology. If there is no information, there is no logic. If you take away all the information from your memory, how will your logic function? It cannot. Information is something that you gather from outside, and the means of gathering this information is only through the five sense organs.

We have gone through this sufficiently: how the sense organs are not reliable, how they are limited, how they perceive only in comparison. You gather certain information; this information is broken into twelve different aspects. So your eyes are not like cameras, as we have always believed. Your eye just grasps information, and it categorizes this information into around twelve different aspects. These different aspects go into different parts of your brain where they all get assimilated, and your brain creates an image. So the way you think the world looks is not the way it is. This is not philosophy, this is not mysticism; this is neurology. The neuroscientists say that if there is no past information about an object in your mind, you actually cannot see it.

Suppose some other kind of person – a kind of person that you have never seen and never imagined – comes and stands here, you most probably will not be able to see him. Anything for which there is no information at all within you, you cannot see that. It is said that when the first European ships went to North America, the native tribes could see the people floating in the ocean and moving toward them, but they could not see the ship. That is because they had never seen a ship before. They had no such information within them, so they could not see it. They say for more than a month they could not see the ship!

You know we have been telling you, whichever way you experience something, it is your karma. Karma means past information. Whichever way your information is, that is the way you see the things right now. So your logic functions based on information. The very nature of information is such that it is always limited, no matter the volume of information you have gathered. There is no such thing as limitless information. When you accumulate a few degrees, when you attach a few more letters of the alphabet to your name, you begin to think – at least some people begin to think – you have got it all. As modern science processes information about the existence around us, we are still not getting any closer to knowing anything. We are more bewildered than any time before.

Before the modern sciences came, in their own simplistic way, people were dead sure of what was what. Now nobody knows anything. So much information has been gathered, but it has not moved you closer to knowing. In fact, it has moved you away from knowing, because that is the nature of existence. Fifty years ago, a doctor was simply a doctor. Twenty-five years ago, a doctor was not just a doctor; there was one doctor for this and one doctor for that, and one doctor for something else. There were three different doctors that your body needed. Today there are over a hundred specialties, so if you really want to be healthy, you need to see a hundred-plus doctors!

I was speaking in Atlanta about a month ago. Just a few days before my talk, I had injured my knee. Then a man – a meditator – popped up and said, "I want to examine your knee." I said, "Why?" He said, "I am a knee doctor." I said, "What? You are an orthopedist?" He said, "No, I am a knee doctor." I said, "What? Are you really a knee doctor? You are just an orthopedist, aren't you? You study bones." He said, "No, I am a knee doctor." "Oh, I didn't know that," I said. Then I asked, "Which knee?" (*Laughter*) Because we are not far off from having one for the right knee and one for the left!

As we study and gather more and more information about life, one day it will happen that for every cell in your body, you will need a different doctor. That is because every cell in the body is so complex that one man cannot grasp it. One human being cannot grasp the whole of what one single cell really is. So you will need a combination of doctors for every cell in your body. As science looks deeper and deeper into life, as scientists gather more and more information, you will see you will become more and more bewildered about life.

One should use information and logic as a drunkard would use a lamp post – only for support, not for illumination. For support it is okay. But if you think it is illuminating the drunkard's life, you are wrong, because anyway he cannot see anything for nuts. Light blurs him out. If you are not ready for the volume of light that is coming your way, it will always blur you out.

So a gnana yogi is not just an intellectual fool. He is not a PhD kind, who is celebrating the volume of information that he has gathered in his life. A gnana yogi understands that his logic, his intellect is a support, but not illumination; he knows that clearly. Logic is like a scalpel. You can open up things, you can use a sharp intellect to cut things open and look inward. By just cutting, you will not know. It is by looking that you will know. Your intellect and logic can only cut; they cannot look. Your logical intellect can do a logical circus, a phenomenal amount of circus.

I want you to know that nowhere else in the world have people used their logic with such devastating impact as they have in Indian culture. This land has seen logic at its ultimate. In the

Vedantic[5] philosophy, logic will rise to such a point that it will just freak you out completely. Not using it like it is done usually, but really using it like a rocket, where it takes you to a place where it makes you dizzy and intoxicated. Then you realize it is not getting anywhere. It just causes dizziness in your head due to excessive use. Then you understand that this can be used only to slice things open. It is not an instrument for seeing.

To see, you need intelligence, and intelligence is not logical. There are many ways to look at this body. One way to look at this body is as a complex chemical factory. There is a certain intelligence which is managing and conducting this whole dance of chemistry. Are you stupid enough to believe that you could someday conduct this whole chemical dance logically? You cannot manage a single cell in your body that way.

So you understand the distinction between the limitation in which the intellect functions and how the intelligence of life functions. What you call intelligence and what you refer to as the Creator are not different. The Creator is just pure intelligence. Intelligence beyond logic is what you are referring to as God. If you operate just within the limitations of your intellectual logic, within the framework of your intellect, you will never know the Creator. You will just do the circus of life. Life is a circus when your intellect and your body alone are involved. But life is a dance when the intelligence begins to play its role.

 "Intuition is not a different dimension of perception... Intuition is just a quicker way of arriving at the same answer."

---

5   Referring to Vedanta: lit. "end of perceivable knowledge"; the philosophy or the teachings of the Upanishads, the speculative and metaphysical commentaries on the Vedas.

Questioner: Does mysticism have something to do with intuition? Is intuition a higher level of perception? Those who use it, are they mystics or mistakes?

Sadhguru: Intuition is not a different dimension of perception, as people usually try to make out. Intuition is just a quicker way of arriving at the same answer. Intuition is just a way of making use of the data and jumping the steps. For example, let's say I ask you, "This year, first of September, what day is it?" What will you do now? You will take a paper and a pen and start calculating. It may take eight to ten steps for you to get there. But anyway these calculations are there in your mind. If you are intuitive, you don't go through those ten steps; you just arrive at the answer. Go to your calculator, and the answer automatically appears. It is not calculating; it is all there. It is able to pull back the information just like that. Similarly, if your mind works like this, you don't have to calculate everything each time; you can just pull out the information needed as and when it is needed. That is intuition.

A lot of children tend to be intuitive. Especially autistic children, who are impaired in some way in terms of normal function, tend to be very intuitive with some other aspect of their minds. Sometime ago I met one boy who was about eleven years of age. He is seriously impaired in many ways and has serious behavioral problems. He is in a special school. But if you ask him, "3000 B.C., March 1st, what day is it?" he will reply right away. If you check it up, it will be right. He will never be wrong. You ask him, "10,000 B.C., September 13th, what is the day?" He will just tell you. (*Laughs*) He does not even have to think about it. It is just there.

So intuition is a different way of arriving at the answer without going through the necessary logical steps. You are skipping the logic and getting there. The logical mind is going through the process; the intuitive mind is not going through the process, but just picking out the information that it wants at the right time. You can be trained for that.

Questioner: Can we train the mind to become more intuitive in our daily lives to make more effective everyday decisions? To what extent do you use intuition, Sadhguru?

Sadhguru: Now, the simple yoga practice that we are teaching here will enhance both logic and intuition. Am I logical? I am. But I don't do anything logically; everything is intuitive for me. That is why it is so effortless. If I had to do all the things that I am doing logically, it would drive me crazy. The volume of activity and the variety of activity that I have taken up in my life would drive people crazy. But because I don't go through it logically, because I arrive at things intuitively, there is no effort in it. It simply happens.

But without data, intuitiveness will not work. You definitely need data. But there is no calculation. And data is gathered every moment; as I said, all the five sense organs are continuously gathering data.

The kind of things that people come to me with is not just spirituality. If somebody is building a building and there is some problem with the engineering, they come to me. If somebody is fixing a machine and there is some problem, they come to me. (*Laughs*) It is not because I am trained in this. It is just that you look at the building, right? If you see this building, whether you are conscious or not conscious, your eyes have taken a complete picture of it. If you want any time, you can pull out that data. If you keep a certain level of clarity, any time you want, it can be pulled out.

If I drive today, especially on the Himalayan range, I know every bend on the road, every rock, every major tree. When I drive, it is like the next corner is already in my mind. People don't understand why I am driving at this speed. Everybody else is traveling at twenty-five to thirty kilometers, and I am just whizzing. This time I went in a Porsche, and I was really blasting it. (*Laughs*) People think I am crazy, but I am already seeing the next two, three bends in the road in my mind. I only have to watch out for the vehicles, I don't have to bother about the road at all because the road is very clear in my mind. And it is so in everybody's mind; it is just that they messed it up so much that they cannot pull out the information when they need it. They are just messing it up inside.

So, as you do the practice, if you are connected with your consciousness, then the mind is just free. It is so free that everything that you have smelled, tasted, touched, heard and seen is all there. You don't have to try to remember anything; it is all simply there. You can just pull it back. Memory is not about remembering, memory is just about your ability to bring back the data, isn't it?

Questioner: So all of us have it to some extent, don't we? – a kind of gut feeling about things? How much importance should we give this intuition?

Sadhguru: See, today these things are completely going away, but in the last generation, if you went to the doctor, the doctor would simply sit and have a conversation with you and know everything that is right and wrong with you. Do you know this? Nobody would scan you with all these MRIs and CATs. A doctor would just sit there, converse with you, just ask you about how your family is going, how your work is going, how your cows are doing, and in the end he would know what is happening with you. Even now there are a few doctors like that. All this information is written on you in so many ways.

If you come to certain parts of South India, you will see certain communities of people that have been traditionally trained in these things. They just look at your face and they will tell you your father's name, your mother's name, your child's name. They will tell you almost everything about what has happened to you in your life and what may happen to you tomorrow. And after all that, they ask you for just ten rupees. For just that ten rupees, he will just tell you everything. You would think it is a great thing, isn't it? That somebody is able to see through you like this. But every day he collects ten rupees from eight to ten people! If they come to our houses, we say, "No, no, already so many people have told me about myself. Go." (*Laughs*) Because there are too many of them.

So this is intuition. If you are willing to look carefully, you know how to use it. Now, sometimes, unconsciously you are able to grasp some information about the other person. Intuition is just using the data in a very beautiful and effective way. But it is not another dimension of perception.

But as I repeatedly keep saying, you can activate different levels of perception in the human system. When I say different levels of perception, I mean that if I sit here with my eyes closed and if somebody walks into the hall from the back, I will tell you what kind of person has entered the hall. This is not any great yoga. Your dog can do it, you know? Your dog is hiding under the sofa; when somebody walks in, he knows who has walked in. You also have it. So why did you lose it? It has been lost because you are too psychological; you are not with the world. You are just too busy with your own nonsense all the time that all the beautiful things that you are capable of have been lost, that's all.

Sometimes intuition is a very confusing thing. A lot of people say, "Oh, I think I have a gut feeling." People who go to the horse races particularly! (*Laughter*) Ninety percent of the time they lose, but still they have a gut feeling because it worked once. It worked once and ten times it failed, but still they go on banking on that one time that worked. That is, just by chance things may happen.

Intuition once in a way is a very dangerous thing because you won't know how to decide whether it is a hundred percent yes or no; so great turmoil will happen within you, yes? Your logical mind says one thing; you think your intuition is saying something else. It must be one hundred percent clear; otherwise intuition is more of a nuisance. It is better to drop it and just rely on the logical process. Even if it takes longer, at least you get somewhere. This intuition may just land you in all kinds of situations because you believe things. There are lots of people like this, who are constantly making wrong decisions about everything in their life because they think they have intuition. If there is even a one percent doubt, it is better to use the logical mind, however limited it is, because it is more reliable. You can cross-check it. Intuition cannot be cross-checked.

 "Work on yourself. Don't worry about God."

Questioner: I have a metaphysical question regarding the connection between the physical body and the mind. Scientifically at least, I guess we are led to believe that the brain is the seat of the mind. Is the mind more than a physical entity? When we speak of the mind, do we mean the discriminating mind? Or do we mean a deeper aspect that is the subconscious? Is any aspect of the mind linked to mysticism? And another question: what happens when someone dies?

Sadhguru: Would you like to know God's email ID as well? (*Laughs*) Now first, I want you to understand this: there is nothing metaphysical about your question. It is just about the physical.

We will answer the question from this end. What will happen after I die? This is a very physical question, because death is a physical matter, isn't it? Death is concerned with the physical body, so it is an issue of the physical. So what you call "mind" is also physical – subtle but still physical. Now you are trying to locate the mind in your body. Do you have a mind? Maybe you don't have one! Do you have a body? See, you know that you have a body, and you know where it is right now. But what about the mind? Are you sure you have a mind?

Questioner: I think so!

Sadhguru: Lots of people think so many things about themselves. Lots of people think that they are very courageous. When they are faced with situations, you know how they will be? Everybody likes to think fanciful things about themselves; that is not the point. Do you have a mind or not?

Questioner: I don't know...

Sadhguru: If you don't even know whether you have one, then what to do? How to locate it? Now, in the English language, everything is passing off as the mind. In yoga, we have divided the different faculties of this dimension that you are referring to as "mind" in different ways: "*chitta*," "*manas*," and "*sakshi*."

"Chit" or "chitta" is the discriminative dimension. So as I mentioned earlier, discrimination cannot function without the sense organs' support. When your sense organs are asleep, there is no discrimination. So that part of the mind functions only with the support of the sense organs. The discriminatory nature of the mind is just an inner extension of the sense perception, a receptive point for all the senses. The senses are information-gatherers; there is a receptive point which is one part of the mind, which gives you the faculty of discrimination.

There is another part of the mind which is called "manas," which can function even when your sense organs are asleep. This dimension is active in your dream states. Your sense organs have gone to sleep, you have no experience of the body or the world, but another part of the mind is just going on by itself. This is manas. This manas came as an empty space. Now whatever you gathered in your chitta, all the information that you gathered in the chitta is reflected in the manas. Now, how it reflects depends on how you keep your manas. If your manas is perfectly still, then it gives you a proper reflection of whatever you have gathered. If your manas is wavy, it gives you a distorted vision of everything. This is the reason why each person perceives the same situation in many, many different ways.

Have you seen those distorted mirrors? You go and look at yourself; maybe that is the reality. (*Laughs*) If we had only distorted mirrors in the world, slowly you would believe, "I am like this." Suppose everywhere in your house and wherever you go, there is a particular distortion to the mirror, gradually you would start thinking, "my face is like this," wouldn't you? So manas is just a mirror. If you keep it still and well-polished, then it just gives you a clear vision of everything the way it is. Otherwise it distorts everything.

Beyond this is a dimension called "sakshi." Sakshi is just witnessing. That dimension of the mind may not be active in you as yet. It is possible, but for most people it is not. For some moments it might have become active. Sakshi means a witness. That means you witness everything, but you are not a part of it. So the many spiritual methods and processes that are being employed around the world – in the form of meditation, prayer, etc. – are to somehow bring some sense of witnessing in you.

People are struggling hard, but most do not get there because they have not done sufficient work either on their sense organs, or on their chitta, or on their manas. They are just trying to handle that end of the mind, and because of this, there are no results. There is only endless struggle. One moment they may experience something, but again the next moment, the same nonsense will be there.

But how can one work on the mind? Let's look at it totally technically. It is true that there is another dimension of subjectivity, which cannot be made technical. But if you do not handle the technical part of it properly, if that dimension is not ready, then even if grace descends upon you, still you will miss it. This is only because you are not receptive enough. So you can work on this. Whatever is in your hands, you keep that in perfect condition; then what is beyond you will anyway happen. But people are always trying to work at what is beyond them, not taking care of what is in their hands.

This is what seeking God means. You are trying to fix God, but you are not seeing how to become receptive. Now, you work on yourself. Don't worry about God. Don't worry about that dimension which is beyond your limitations. Your business is to work with the limitations and fine-tune them to such a point that what is beyond limits cannot avoid you. It has to come to you.

So, that is the method that I am talking about, to put it very technically. If you prepare your sense perception, your discriminative function and the reflecting aspect of the mind (the manas), then undistorted vision is there. Witnessing naturally arises. Once witnessing arises, slowly becoming free from the process of body and process of mind becomes natural.

You take care of these things and what has to happen will happen. Things do not descend upon anything that is not ready to receive them. Even if the rain falls, the sunlight falls, will the rocks sprout? The seed will sprout, isn't it? But a rock just sits there. The rock does not know what sunlight is; it does not know what rain is. That is not because rain and sunlight are missing it, but simply because a rock is incapable of knowing. There is nothing wrong with a rock; it is just not receptive to those things. Similarly, there is nothing wrong in being unenlightened and stupid. It is just that it is so limited.

Now once you are in a human form, a certain sprout of intelligence has come in you, which will bother you if you are limited. It will not let you rest, isn't it? So, because this intelligence bothers you, you eat more, you drink more, you lust more, you do everything more, just to see that your intelligence does not bother you and tell you that you are stupid. If you do not do any of those things, if you just sit quietly for three days and look at your life, you will feel utterly stupid. But you kept yourself so busy that there was no time to see or identify your stupidity, isn't it? Now suddenly after this yoga you feel so utterly stupid, but blissful. It is nice. (*Laughs*)

"If you are fanatical about what you believe in, you cannot be confused. Or if you are realized, you cannot be confused. Between ignorance and enlightenment is a very thin line."

Questioner: But how can we sustain this witnessing of the self through the maze of our emotions and thoughts?

Sadhguru: The question of sustaining something comes up only after it has come into your experience, isn't it? As I have mentioned before, the very nature of the intellect is that it needs division to perceive anything. The mind is always going about dividing everything into good and bad: "I like this, I don't like this." There have to be two polarities for the mind to perceive anything. What you are referring to as the "self" has no polarities. There is only one. "One" cannot be perceived by the mind or by the sense perceptions. Both the sense organs and the mind always need two to perceive, because the mind can perceive things only in comparison.

See, without a polarity, without duality, the mind is a useless instrument. Only when there is duality, the mind works. That is the mind's field of activity. If there is no duality, the mind will split it into two. This is the nature of the intellect: it is constantly discriminating. So, as I said earlier, the intellect is like a knife which cuts everything into pieces, because without the two, it cannot function. Therefore the whole dimension of what we refer to as the "spiritual" is to transcend duality so that there is only one, not two. The word "yoga" literally means union. That means everything has become one.

How can everything become one? Have you heard of a word called "samadhi?" Samadhi literally means this: "sama" means equanimous, and "dhi" refers to the "buddhi" or the intellect. It means you have made the intellect equanimous, or you have transcended the intellect in such a way that it is not discriminating anymore. Once the discrimination stops, then in your experience there is no "me" and no "other," no "you" and "me." Once there is no "you" and "me," there is no such thing as thought. There is no such thing as emotion. It goes beyond that. You may ask, "Is samadhi a thoughtless, emotionless, dry state?" It is not dry. It is the very source of creation.

So, "witnessing the self" is very misleading terminology. It might have been said from a certain experience, because words cannot describe this. Language is always about two. If there is no duality, there is no language. Language can be very eloquent about describing all the aspects of life, but about the oneness of the existence, it is useless. So, if you try to talk about this "oneness," whichever way you attempt to say it, you are creating duality with language. That is the reason why the Eastern spiritual sciences always use negative terminology. This minimizes the imagination. If we use positive terminology, too much imagination will happen. If you say "God," people will start imagining all kinds of gods. If you say "Kingdom of God," they will start imagining all kinds of fancy things in their heads. So the Eastern spiritual processes always use negative terminology. Now we say "shoonya," or emptiness. Not much room left for the imagination, is there? (*Laughs*) So Gautama, the Buddha, said "nirvana." Nirvana means non-existence. He is also talking about emptiness in a different way. He speaks not of "*atma*" but "*anatma*"; that means "non-self." We say "*nirkaya*;" that means no-body. So, why all these negative terms are used is to get as close to the truth as possible with language. Because whichever way you use language, language belongs to the world of duality. Language can never describe something that is all-encompassing.

Now, when you say "witnessing the self," that means you are separate and the self is separate. The moment you talk about a witness, you are talking about you being something other than the self. So once again, you have a problem. Self means "you," isn't it? How do you witness the self? The mind can play tricks with you, as if it is witnessing. There is no witnessing like that. The self *is* witnessing; that is a closer and more accurate way of putting it. But that is confusing, isn't it? "Witnessing is the self" and "the self is witnessing;" there is no separation between the two. If you are witnessing the self, who is the "you?" That leads to confusion. You are simply complicating things with words. However many words you use, it does not matter. Words do not get you there.

So, sustaining the witnessing of the self becomes even worse, because then you are constantly in that misunderstanding. Now, instead of trying to witness the self, the whole effort here is to crank up your energies in such a way that if you sit here, you can witness the mind, and you can witness the body. If you separate the mind and the body from yourself, you are witnessing the mind and body, but you are not witnessing the self. The self is witnessing the mind and body. Now that is a different thing.

The mind can imagine many things. So, people start describing the shape of the self, the size of the self, you know? It is happening. It is happening in a huge way around the world, because the mind cannot grasp anything unless there is a shape and size to it. It needs some description. This is the reason why people always ask, "Can you define God?" This is because the mind needs a definition for everything. Without it, the mind cannot grasp anything. Much has been said about these things. Those who know will not speak about it; those who do not know always speak about it. Huge books have been written about it. They have been revered in big ways around the world, but that does not matter. That which cannot be divided cannot be described or defined either.

So do not try to witness the self. Witness your body, witness your mind. You are the self. What you call "me" is the self. Right now maybe what you call "me" is just your personality. So that is the whole effort: to take the experience of life beyond your personality, to see that personality is something that you created. Once you are aware that you have created it, you can create it whichever way you want. You do not have to be stuck with it one way or the other. In every given situation, you can be a different kind of personality. What is the problem with that?

For instance, people are constantly confused about me. It is okay. Confusion is a good state to be in. It means you are looking, constantly looking. If you arrive at a conclusion, there will be no more looking. People ask me, "Why do you confuse us like this?" I want you to understand, if you can be confused by anybody, it means you do not know. If you are fanatical, you cannot be confused. Or if you are realized, you cannot be confused. Between ignorance and enlightenment is a very thin line. But they are worlds apart.

 "If they are demanding your money or your property, it is not worth it. You must go only to that place where they are demanding your life."

Questioner: How does one differentiate between real mysticism and the superstition and fraudulence that masquerade as mysticism? How do we recognize a true spiritual master, an authentic guru?

Sadhguru: How to differentiate what is counterfeit and what is real? It is a hard job because sometimes the counterfeit looks better than the real thing. (*Laughs*) So, there must be some way. First, you must see, what is it doing to you? That is the question.

What experiences you have had, what you have seen, if you have seen God – all that does not mean anything. You saw God. So what the hell? What has it done to you? What is the transformation it has left in you? That is the question. Has it in some way transformed you into a more joyful, more intense human being? Have you become a better life? Better, not in terms of morality, but just as life, have you taken a step within you? If it is so, even if it is fake, what is the problem? Use it.

Suppose they are willing to accept the counterfeit in shops, what is your problem? You use it if it works. Sometimes for small periods of time it may work, but it is best to look at it. What is it that they are demanding out of you? If they are demanding your money or your property, it is not worth it. You must go only to that place where they are demanding your life. If they are demanding anything less than that, they are no good. They will not be any good to you. Someone who demands your life, he is good. What can he do with your life anyway? (*Laughs*) Yes? Tell me, what can I do with your life? But I demand life, nothing less than that. Let's suppose you say, "No, I will go to the other place where if I give ten rupees, everything is okay," then you are going to a fake place. They must demand your life.

So if they are demanding anything less than your life, you can conclude they are a fake. But we do not have to make that judgment. You can go on and see if it is bringing about some transformation. You can go on some more, but with a little caution. Then if they try to con you, you can always step out. Even the conman initially doles out stuff. You take that and walk out. They usually give you a free sample. (*Laughter*) When you go to the mall, initially they give you a free sample of something. You eat it and come. What is your problem? They won't poison you, because poisoning is not good for the future sales, is it? (*Laughter*)

The fake will never dare to demand your life because they are afraid you may not give it. Do you understand? They are afraid you may not give it. If you give your life, what can I do with it? That is not the point. If you give it, I don't get it. It is just that it puts you into that attitude of absolute giving. That transforms you. That attitude of "I will give away my life to you" makes the difference. Can I take it in a bag and go somewhere? I cannot take it. But the fact that you are willing to give away your life – that completely changes you. It completely changes your life.

Questioner: But how do we address the problems of corrupt gurus, the fake mystics, who take advantage of people?

Sadhguru: Certain unfortunate incidents have happened. They have happened because in terms of the media, society and the general situation in the country, we have still not set up a certain amount of quality control. Just about anybody can sell anything, anybody can do anything. This is hugely maligning the spiritual content of this country. One of the greatest assets we have in India is our spiritual knowledge. The depth of knowledge that we have, in terms of an understanding of the human mechanism, is phenomenal. Yes, some have handled it irresponsibly in the name of the spiritual process, and have damaged peoples' lives. That has unfortunately happened.

But if you buy a basket of mangoes, and find that one mango is rotten, what will you do? Quickly pull out that mango and throw it away? Or give up eating mangoes? You won't give up the sweetness of the mango, will you? So because we found one rotten mango, we need not give up the sweetness of the spiritual process. We must quickly dispose of it, forget about it and focus on what needs to be done.

But unfortunately, or maybe that is the way of the world today, our focus is too much on the negative that is happening. So many thousands of gurus are doing fantastic work but they never get any press. But because of somebody who is into some sleaze or gets into some scandal, the world is made to feel that all the gurus are like this. There are corrupt politicians, there are corrupt doctors, there are corrupt press people, there are corrupt police officers, and there are corrupt spiritual people. This does not mean there is no good work happening. There is a phenomenal amount of good work happening. It is just that a few people are corrupt. If you find one policeman to be corrupt and you think all police officers are corrupt, it is not true. The country would not be in one piece if the entire police force were corrupt.

But that does not mean corruption should be taken lightly. Especially when it comes to the spiritual arena, it needs to be handled more strictly because this is an area of life that people have to approach with a certain level of trust. If a shopkeeper cheats you of something, it is only a loss of money; it is not good, but you can afford to ignore it. But if a doctor deceives you, then it is a question of your life, and it becomes a big thing. If a spiritual guru deceives you, your trust and much deeper things in your life are disturbed. So when it comes to a spiritual guru or your doctor, where life and death are involved, trust is a very essential part of it; any misuse of that has to be handled severely.

I would tell people to choose carefully. Don't blindly rush into something, then get hurt and come back. It is best that people choose more carefully.

CHAPTER 2

BREAKING THE BUBBLE
From Limitation to Life

"The spiritual process is not about being ethical or moral, good or bad. It is just looking for ways to break the limitations in which we exist."

"If one can just sit here, one becomes like the Creator; a piece of creation naturally transforms itself into the Creator."

Sadhguru: The word "spirituality" is one of the most corrupted words on the planet. It has been used and misused in a million different ways, largely because of ignorance, and often out of unscrupulousness. It has generated such a level of confusion and doubt in people's minds as to whether it is really worthwhile or not. It has created a phenomenal amount of uncertainty. Even after walking the path for many years, people have doubts, because there has been such ambiguity and such a level of misunderstanding.

It is important to remember that whatever goes on in our minds cannot be spiritual. If you think about God, that is not spiritual. If you think about heaven, that is not spiritual. If you think about liberation, that is not spiritual either. Thought is essentially psychological; there is nothing spiritual about it.

This little finger is physical. If I say this is spiritual, then there will be a whole lot of confusion attached to it. This little finger is plain physical. Maybe I have made my physical system in such a way that my little finger, or my whole body, or at least one cell in my body, has become a conducive passage for a spiritual process. It is possible, but still it is not spiritual. It is a good physical little finger. It can be a block or it can be a gate, but still it is physical.

The physical is not against the spiritual. It is only because we have a physical body that we are thinking of another dimension. If we did not exist here physically, the need for the spiritual process would never have arisen anywhere at all. So the physical is, in a way, the basis of the spiritual, but the physical can never become spiritual. Similarly, the psychological can never become spiritual; the emotional can never become spiritual. They are different dimensions of life. Nothing right or wrong about them; it all depends on how you use them. We can use this body as a barrier and a trap, or we can use this body as a passage. Similarly, we can use this mind as a misery-manufacturing machine, or we can use it as a spiritual possibility. But mind, body, emotions – these things cannot be spiritual.

When we say "spiritual," we are talking about a dimension which does not belong to this realm. If all we are looking for is peace, then that is not spirituality. People are talking about spiritual peace; there is no such thing. Peace is of the physical and the mental. You can disturb the physical, you can disturb the psychological, but you cannot disturb that which is neither of these two things. So the spiritual is neither seeking peace, nor does it need peace.

When we say "spirituality," we are talking about a dimension which is not yet in one's perception. This integrated mechanism of body, mind, emotions and the physical energy – these four things together have made this being physical. Now this and the rest of existence is made of the same material, but because of its integrity – the way it is constructed – this mechanism looks absolutely individual right now. It is so perfectly individual that you cannot believe this person and that person could be one. Every being is just the five elements. You are just water, earth, air, fire and space; that is all you are. The same five elements have become such a fantastic amalgamation that it has become a human being right now. What you are is just the play of these five elements, but the play is so beautifully constructed that it is complete by itself, and it can exist alone up to a point.

See, when we begin to question the very existence of the Creator that means the creation is perfect. If every day it could not function without morning and evening prayers, then this would not be a perfect creation. This creation is so perfect that you can forget the Creator – you can just discard him, dump him – and still it goes on. So a true compliment to the Creator is when you forget about him. (*Laughs*) That is a real compliment to the wonderful piece of creation he has made; it is so perfect within itself that it does not need to draw from anything outside.

The problem is people will forget God, but they will lean on something else. If they do not lean on anything else, if they just sit here and don't look for anything from the outside – a relationship or psychological help, emotional help, nothing – then something wonderful can happen. If one can just sit here, one becomes like the Creator. A piece of creation naturally transforms itself into the Creator.

The problem is we play every game halfheartedly. If you play any one game totally, you will break the limitations of your existence. All the time we play games – sometimes spiritual, sometime material, sometimes this way, sometimes that way. But if you play any one thing a hundred percent fully, you will be there in no time. I keep telling people, "You don't know meditation; don't worry! You don't know love; don't worry! You don't know peace; don't worry! Just be angry; you know how to be angry. Just sustain your anger for twenty-four hours, with maximum intensity, and you will become enlightened. That is all it takes."

Just stay on one thing. But the very way people are made right now is, they cannot stay on any one thing; they constantly keep shifting. Have you ever been angry for twenty-four hours? Have you ever been miserable for twenty-four hours? You think you have been, but it is not so. In between, thoughts go off somewhere else, to something else; there is respite. Do not give yourself respite; just stay on something for twenty-four hours, and you are there. You cannot meditate, but you could be angry, or at least you could be miserable. If you do not know anything else, try it and see; it will work. (*Laughs*) It does work. It you just stick to something in an unmoving way for twenty-four hours, things will happen; things will explode. See, it is like this: you go underwater, and you let out one bubble at thirty meters below the water. It is only a small bubble. But as it goes up, as the pressure decreases it becomes such a big bubble. Just the tiny, compressed bubble that you let out there becomes so big when it goes up. It is like an explosion; you cannot believe it.

Or just blow bubbles in the air. The inside of the bubble and the outside of the bubble are made of the same stuff, but still the bubble has a distinct identity. So this individual nature is just like that: the inside and the outside are the same stuff. But there is just one little crafty barrier – such a crafty barrier, you cannot even see it. Whichever way you look at it, there seems to be no barrier. But there is a distinct barrier between the individual and the rest, isn't it? It does not matter how hard you try, the barrier is still there. You tell somebody, "I love you," but the next moment you are thinking, "Okay, what about this guy? (*Laughs*) Is he all right or not?" So it is just made out of the same material – water inside water, air inside air, mud inside mud. But the distinction is so beautifully crafted that you can never grasp it.

So if we want to know this piece of life, there is one approach. If we want to cross it, there is another approach. But for one who does not break the barriers, there is no possibility of knowing. First breaking the barrier and then knowing is a much longer process. If you just want to enjoy the freedom and bliss of crossing the barrier – which is much simpler than knowing, because knowing takes much more time – all it takes is an intense direction towards any one thing. This is not possible for people who are multi-tasking. (*Laughs*) That is a very common word I am hearing these days; everybody is "multi-tasking."

If one wants to go somewhere, one has to stick to one thing. This is why all the devotees on the planet look like crazy nuts. Since they are just stuck on to the object of their devotion they look like nut cases for the rest of the world. For somebody looking at them from outside, they look absolutely unintelligent and lost. They look brainwashed. This has always been the way: many took to a single approach because their goal was only spiritual. They had no social involvement, nor did they care. If it is so, it is fine. But always these people were persecuted – always.

Have you heard of Mansur Al-Hallaj? He was born in Persia in the ninth century. It is said that he was a learned man who went east to teach. He first went to Gujarat in India. There he met some genuine loonies (*Laughs*) who were in a completely different state of bliss. And from there he went a little farther up into Punjab. There he met lots of them, and after a few years of being there, he came back to his land, wanting to share this. When he came back, it was in a loincloth. In the society he came from, a man walking around in the street in a loincloth was simply, utterly crazy. He not only came in this almost naked condition, but he was also saying, "I am nothing; I am nobody," and started singing and dancing madly on the street. People distanced themselves from him, seeing he had gone crazy, but still some were drawn to him.

Now, he had come to an ecstatic state within himself. See, when you become very ecstatic, on one level what is happening is that what was an integrated structure becomes loose. Or in other words, what was a burnt pot has now become un-burnt: it has become malleable, and you can reshape it whichever way you want. Have you noticed when people are joyful, they are flexible? Yes? When they are unhappy, they are absolutely rigid – rigid as sticks. If you attempt to bend them a little bit, they will break. When they are happy, they are flexible. When they become utterly blissful, they are malleable. When they have

become like that, you can just make them into a ball of mud
and reshape them whichever way you want.

That is why we talk about bliss. We are not some kind of
addicts looking for bliss. We are talking about bliss because
that is a state where a human being becomes malleable. You
can make anything out of him or you can make nothing out of
him. Until he becomes like that, this individual form cannot be
broken down. You can believe many things about yourself –
you can think of many things, have so many emotions – but
after sometime you are back once again to square one. This is
the experience of millions of people on the spiritual path; they
go sit and meditate and they think, "This is it." Two days later,
they are just the same. They go into a beautiful place; they go
into a retreat, and they feel beautiful. But when they come out
on the street again, everything is the same. This is because
unless you take yourself to such an utterly insane state of
ecstasy, you do not become malleable enough to completely
reshape who you are. It will not happen.

Most of the time, it is just on the surface that people are
changing their attitudes. Changing your attitudes is not
spirituality; it is just social nonsense. Having values, having
ethics, may make you into a good man; it may make you into a
pleasant person; it may make you into a socially useful person.
If these things are important for you, it is fine. But you do not
have to call it spirituality.

The spiritual process means that in some way you have
liberated yourself from the bubble, that your individuality is no
more a demarcated area. Once you are not within the
demarcated area, on one level, we can say you are free. On
another level, it is also a tremendous freedom to create
anything that you want, because the very fundamentals of life
are in your hands. You can make anything that you want
around you or within you or anywhere in the world. Suddenly
there is no limitation of time and space. One can work and do
things, irrespective of where one is. If this capability has to
come, the first and foremost thing is to get into ecstatic states –
absolutely mindless ecstasy.

It is in search of this that many people went, but because they were not willing to put in what it takes, they chose drugs. It gave them a false sense of freedom. The problem is the moment the effect of the drug is over, the presence of the trap is so very strong. Artificially, chemically, you escape for some time; but when you return, you feel the trap of this body and mind like never before. It now becomes such a deep experience. This is why when people chemically create some sense of freedom, you will notice that when they do not have that support anymore, they will become utterly miserable. Whether it is through alcohol or drugs or whatever else, if they experience some sense of freedom without creating the necessary awareness for it, the sense of despondency is so huge that it breaks them up. Lots of people who went into ecstatic states in artificial ways ended up with broken minds, simply because they could not bear being trapped once again. Those who have always lived in the trap, they do not feel it so much. It is people who have known the freedom and come back, who feel it terribly. It is terrible to be back once again. Unless you have built your own ladder to climb out at will, just escaping by chance generally leads to broken minds; people get psychologically broken.

So the essence of the spiritual process needs to be understood as a means to generate the necessary intensity to break the bubble, so that you are out of your individual nature. It is not about being good, it is not about being ethical, it is not about being moral. These things may all happen as a result, as a consequence. Once you have broken the bubble and known the freedom of experiencing everything as yourself, as a consequence you may function as a good person in society. But you have no particular intention of being good!

Does that sound very bad? See, having the intention of being good means you are essentially bad, isn't it? Now, suppose you have no intention of being good, but whatever you do, people say it is wonderful. I have no idea whether what I am doing is good or bad; I do whatever I have to. I do not have to plan to be good all the time. The idea of somebody being good to somebody, or bad to somebody, has come simply because of the individual nature of who you are. The walls are so strong that being inside this wall you cannot know or you cannot feel that the other is you. Because of that you have to have a good intention; otherwise you will naturally cause harm. There is the instinct of self-preservation which is always thinking of one's own well-being and nothing else. When this disappears, when the wall is down, you do not have to think about your well-being or anybody else's well-being. You simply act as life should act; everything will be just in place.

This person is just a piece of life. If this piece of life functions as a little larger life, everything will be just fine. A plant never thought of giving you beautiful flowers; I want you to know this. Do not have such fancy ideas that "the flowers are blooming for me." They are not blooming for you; it is their nature. They are programmed to be like that. If you water the plant, give it sunlight, it blooms. It has no good intentions or bad intentions. It just blossoms because that is its nature. Similarly, whatever is the nature of this one (referring to oneself), if you nurture it, it will blossom and find its original nature. In that there will be no harm to anybody.

More evil has happened on this planet with good intentions than with bad intentions. Generally, the most horrible things on the planet have always happened with good intentions. People who did the most horrible things on the planet always believed that they were doing great things. Without conviction, how long can you sustain it? You have to believe that you are doing the best thing, only then you can sustain it and endure that nonsense forever.

So the spiritual process is not about being ethical, moral, good or bad. It is just looking for ways to break the limitations in which we exist. What is beyond the limitations, you do not even care whether it is good or bad. Suppose you break these limitations and get out, and let us say the whole existence is the Devil, it should be okay with you. Some would like to believe, "No, no, if I break the limitations, God is waiting." Not necessarily! Who knows what the hell is waiting? Whatever is waiting, whatever is sustaining this existence, whatever its nature, it must be fine with us, isn't it? Whatever is the source of life cannot be against life. It is as simple as that. Is it good or is it bad? It is neither good nor bad. It is just like electricity. Is electricity good or bad? The moment I ask that, everybody says, "It is good, because it is right now heating the place, keeping us warm, and lighting up the place." But stick your finger into the socket and see. Then you will say, "Oh! It's bad!"

It so happened that Shankaran Pillai's mother-in-law's birthday was fast approaching and his wife kept on asking, "What gift shall we give her this year?"

Every day he just kept ignoring her. Then when the birthday was coming close, she really put the pressure on. "What gift shall we buy?"

So Shankaran Pillai said, "Last year we gave her a nice chair. This year we can electrify it for her." (*Laughter*)

Electricity is a good thing. (*Laughs*) Do you have a son-in-law? (*Laughter*) No?

Audience Member: A daughter-in-law.

Sadhguru: Then for sure! (*Laughter*)

Instead of just finding simple methods to break barriers, we have made the so-called "spirituality" in the world so complicated, with all kinds of beliefs and morals and ethics, that it is impossible for any human being to live like that – simply impossible because it is so contradictory.

Once it happened. A Jewish man was crossing the street in front of a Catholic Church and a hit-and-run driver ran him over and went away. The man was lying on the street, almost dead, but still conscious. Then the Catholic priest, who never misses an opportunity like this, ran out of the church, went to him and got busy trying to perform the last rites. He asked him, "Do you believe in God, his Son Jesus and the Holy Ghost?" The man said, "I am dying and you are asking me riddles." (*Laughter*)

So what is a simple straightforward process has unfortunately been made into such a horrible riddle that nobody can figure it out, and people are taking enormous pleasure in saying it cannot be figured out. People are now talking about how to make God happy, how to make God peaceful. (*Laughter*) They say, "If you do this and this, God will be happy." If the guy is unhappy we must get rid of him! Maybe only because of his unhappiness the whole world is suffering. (*Laughs*) So people know how to make God happy, but they do not know how to be happy themselves. They know how to make God peaceful, but they do not know how to be peaceful themselves. They know everything about God, but not an iota about themselves. This kind of deceptive way of doing things has unnecessarily made everything into a riddle. It is not even complex. At least if it was complex, we could have enjoyed it intellectually. But it is actually quite a silly riddle.

It is said that when Mansur came back from India, people thought he was crazy. And the final straw was when he said, "I am God." Then he had it. (*Laughs*) The moment he said, "I am God," he was accused of many things. As if that was not enough, he went to Mecca. Everybody was going round the Kaaba[6] there. He thought, "Why such a big rush? Why are all you guys going around here?" And he set up another one. Most probably he consecrated it, and he saw that both of them embodied the same energy. He told people, "Why should everybody go around one stone? It is too crowded. You can go around this." That was the last straw.

So for that he was tortured and publicly crucified. Some say they actually peeled off his skin alive, that his hands and feet were cut off and he was beheaded. There is a story that the

---

6   A cuboid shaped building which pilgrims circumambulate counterclockwise. Located in the Grand Mosque in Mecca.

local caliph gave an order that anybody who passes that street must throw a stone at him. You could not pass without throwing a stone. When his dear friend, Shibli, was passing that way, he also had to throw something. But he did not have the heart to throw a stone, so he threw a flower at him. Then Mansur burst into poetry, and he said, "Of all the things, those stones don't hurt me because they are thrown by the ignorant. But you, you threw this flower – this has hurt me so deeply, because although you know, you have still thrown something at me."

So it is extremely important if we want to walk the spiritual path that we learn to keep the mind and emotion in a certain level of stability, and let the rest of it go utterly crazy. If madness does not happen, then there is nothing new happening; we have not broken anything. What we call "mad" is someone who has become different from the way we know life, isn't it? Someone has become different. He has crossed the barriers. Usually madness happens when he somehow breaks what you cannot break. It does not matter what kind of circus is happening in your life, still there is one part of your mind which is thinking clearly. When that goes away, you are mad. If that does not go away, you will never know moments of ecstasy, you will never know moments of love, you will never know moments of utter peace. If that part of your mind does not go away, you will not know meditation, you will not know love, you will not know dance, you will not know music. You will not know anything of life. You will only know body and mind. So, you will remain a BMW: Body, Mind and the World! That is all you will know. (*Laughs*) If something beyond has to happen, somehow the logical thinking has to go.

"But if that goes," you wonder, "will I become insane?" No, normally what we know as madness is insanity; that is not the madness that I am talking about. That insanity has happened not because logical thinking is gone, but because it has become unreasonable logic. An insane person believes that he is very logical; he thinks others are not logical. Isn't it so? Do you notice how strongly insane people will argue because they believe they are logical? Their logic has not gone. It has just gotten twisted, but it is still very, very strong. If it had gone, they would be realized. But it has not gone.

Generally, in English, one way in which we describe an insane person is like this: "He is out of his mind." See, if you were out of your mind, would you be insane? Insanity is of the mind always, isn't it? Only if you are in the mind you can be insane. If you are out of your mind, you will be perfectly sane; you will become like a Mansur, or a Jesus or someone who is beyond other people's understanding. Others may think they are insane, but they are the only few sane people that have happened on the planet.

So, if such sanity comes, there will be no logic left in you. Enlightenment is beyond logic; there is no logic there. You cannot mess with it anymore, because there is nothing to mess with. If there was something, you could ruin it. There is nothing, so you cannot ruin it. When there is nothing, then everything flows through you. Whatever has to happen in this existence, it has to flow through you. You become the gateway. There is nothing that can escape your grasp, if you are willing. If you have the inclination, everything is within your grasp.

 "When you are on the spiritual path you do not think about mastery; you think about freedom."

Questioner: If everything and everyone – including me and you – is just an amalgamation of the five elements, what does it mean to have mastery over them? Is it possible to totally master them, and by implication, gain mastery over ourselves?

Sadhguru: Oh, if you have total mastery over water, we can convert all the bathrooms into bedrooms. (*Laughter*) If you have total mastery over earth, we can close down the kitchen. If you have total mastery over air, we can keep you in a vacuum. Like this, we can go on, but what is the point? There is still enough air in the world to breathe. When such a day comes when there is no air left, we will teach you such things. There is no such danger yet. We are getting there, but not yet.

Any technology is valuable only because it is relevant to that time. Otherwise, it is irrelevant. So if you talk about mastery, there are many things you can do, because, as I said, the whole existence, as you know it, is only the five elements. If you have mastery, you can play with this existence in many different ways. But when you are on the spiritual path, you do not think about mastery; you think about freedom. You think of how to become free from the five elements. The bondage of life is through the five elements and the possibility of life is also through the five elements. The fundamental ingredient of human life is freedom. So the spiritual process only thinks of liberation, not of mastery.

If you become a master of something, you can do one kind of circus in the world. Maybe if you have the mastery over the water element, you can walk upon water. Then what? If you walk across the ocean, then you must know how to walk on the land once again. If you are constantly walking upon water (*Laughs*) and you don't know how to walk on land, you will end up in a fishy neighborhood, isn't it? So mastery is not what we are looking for. To be free from the five elements is what we are looking for, because the very composition of the body is the five elements. The very existence which binds you and holds you is also made of the five elements.

You need to understand freedom and bondage are two edges of the same sword. If you swing it this way, it is freedom; if you swing it that way, it is bondage. The whole process of life is like this. Love and hate are encapsulated in each other. Life and death are included in each other. If they were separate, you could have easily dealt with them, but they are always within each other. If you try to avoid death, the only thing that you will end up avoiding is life. Please see this: if you just create this within yourself that "I don't want to die, I don't want to die, I don't want to die," all that will happen is that you will not step out of your bed. The only thing you will avoid is life, not death.

This is the way life is; everything is one inside the other. If they were all starkly separate, it would be very simple, and by now you would have been done with life. What you call "space" is not geography; it is just the projection of your consciousness. What you call "time" and "space" are projections of your consciousness. So what is there is here also; what is here is there also. What is that is this also; what is this is that also. Everything is one inside the other. Above all, if you look at it, everything is just within you. It seems to be so complex, but at the same time it is absolutely simple.

The seeming elaborateness of life confuses people. In ancient India there were courtesans who were supposed to be masters in the art of luring people in a certain way towards their own end. So they wore elaborate jewelry. Their whole body was covered in jewels and there was no way to take them off. If you had to take them off one by one, it would take many hours. So, the man, who is fired up by lust, wants to undress this woman, but he cannot take the jewels off. So she will go on encouraging him with a little more liquor or whatever else – a little more, and a little more. And as his vision gets a little more blurred, this whole thing gets even more difficult, and then he will give up and fall asleep. So he falls asleep and starts snoring, never realizing that there is just one pin here (*pointing to his chest*). If you just pull this one pin, everything falls down. That only she knows. (*Laughs*) So, life is just like that. It is one complex web. But there is just one simple pin – if you pull that, everything will just fall. It is as simple as that. And that pin is you. If you know how to pull yourself out, suddenly everything settles. Everything is crystal clear.

This happened in Pennsylvania in the 1890s. Pennsylvania was known for its floods and a flood happened which was quite devastating. So a reporter went there, sat on top of a tree, and looked at what happened. Then he went to the nearest place where he could send his message to his editor and he started saying, "On this day God sat upon the mountain and just watched the valley filling up, as homes went under..." Like this he went about poetically describing the flood, and he sent this to his editor. Instantly, the editor shot back a message: "Forget about the flood. Interview God!"

So you are missing the point. The play of the five elements is so complex; at the same time, the key is you. The core of you is the key. If you pull the plug, it just collapses and you are free from it. If you want to gain mastery over it, then you have to ask yourself what it is that you are seeking. Do you want to walk upon water or do you want to walk upon air or do you want to do some other feat? "I did not eat for fifteen days, do you know?" There are lots of people saying this in a country where there are many people who have not eaten well their whole life. So what is the big deal about it?

So you eating or not eating, walking upon water, holding your breath for a long period of time or whatever kind of mastery you gather over the five elements, only leads to a certain kind of circus which may impress some people, but not me. I will not be impressed, nor is this existence impressed. But if you become free from these five elements, then you live a truly blessed life here, because they do not rule you anymore. This is not mastery; this is just freedom.

I hope you understand the distinction. We are not trying to control existence; we want to become free from it, so that we can really enjoy the way it is and also go beyond that. So we have not set up instruments of mastery here. I have wasted a couple of lifetimes doing that, and yes, it does give you power. But it is not worth it.

Questioner: I understand that freedom from the elements is more important than mastery. But something I have always wondered about is levitation. Is it really possible for yogis to do this? Or is it a myth? If it is possible, can you explain how it happens? And can you levitate, Sadhguru?

Sadhguru: (*Laughs*) Is it possible? It is possible. How does it happen? There are certain ways through which you can become less and less available to gravity. There are practices – kriyas – through which this can happen. Because of this, one may levitate; it is possible. Or, when your *kundalini*[7] rises with tremendous force, you may not levitate, but you can see your body just taking off by itself and landing. It does not stay up there, but it takes off and lands, takes off and lands. With my own eyes I have seen people in cross-legged positions cover fifty to sixty feet in one leap. Just one leap! There are those who could win an Olympic gold medal in long jump, just sitting. With a little effort when the energy is high, it happens.

Have you heard of Mayamma, the woman saint in Tamil Nadu? Nobody knew where she came from, but her features suggested that she was Nepalese. She never spoke. She lived in Kanyakumari, the very tip of Southern India. Her friends were dogs. She had a whole band of dogs behind her. She was so involved with these dogs that she would steal food from hotels for them. You know these small hotels where they keep these *vadas* and other things? She would just go grab them and feed them to her dogs. So many times people mishandled her, even physically. They would beat her and throw stones at her because she grabbed food from everybody and gave it to the dogs. Then some people who went and watched her found that at certain times she would be just sitting and floating on the waves of the ocean. She would sit on the ocean and simply start floating. And so gradually, people stopped bothering her. They would protect their food, of course, but they would not abuse her physically after that.

There are many ways you can make yourself less available to gravity. Can I do it? I want to walk on the planet. I have no intention of floating! Certainly there are people who follow

---

7   Lit. serpent power. Cosmic energy, symbolized as a snake coiled at the base of the spine, that through the practice of yoga, rises upward.

the path of *hata yoga*[8] who can do these feats. It is of no life-significance. Now, if you float or if you levitate for a few minutes in a day, in what way does it alter your life?

Our whole effort here is to make sure that you walk through life very much on the ground. It is to make sure that you can walk through life. No matter what happens with your life, no matter what kind of situations you face, you go through life untouched, like a child, as if you are just born. However many things happen in your life, it does not matter. Even if everything goes dead wrong and every day is a crisis, you still go untouched through life. This is a miracle. I want all of you to perform this miracle. On your deathbed, if you are the way you were when you were just born, that means you have performed a wonderful miracle. It is possible. And that is the miracle we are interested in.

Floating in the air, walking upon the water – what will you do with it? For three days if you walk upon the water, it will be fine when you get all the attention. But every day if you start walking on the water, nobody will look at you. They will all take out their speed boats, and then you will also wish you had one, isn't it?

 "If you want to be sensitive to life, you must be life yourself."

Questioner: You have said that one has to be "life sensitive" to experience higher dimensions of perception. What is this sensitivity? Is it something that one has to be born with or can it be cultivated? If so, how? Are mystics born or made?

---

8 Physical form of yoga involving different bodily postures and practices. Used as both a purificatory and preparatory step for meditation and higher dimensions of spiritual experience.

Sadhguru: Should one be born with this? You have definitely noticed, by birth between one child and another, though we would like to see all children as same, they are not same. They are different. Right from the moment of birth, how they behave, how they cry, how they crawl, how they move their hands, how they look, they are different. It is just foolish to think they are all same. They are as different as grown-ups are, aren't they? Someone is born one way and somebody else another way – one with a certain sense of capability, another without that sense. But is life sensitivity decided by birth alone? Definitely not.

Birth may decide some things. You can take the pole position and still crash your car, isn't it? You can take the pole position and still finish last. You can be in the last and still finish first; it is possible. So birth definitely sets a certain pitch, but it is not the deciding factor. Life is the deciding factor. You are talking about life sense, so definitely life is the deciding factor.

How to become sensitive to life? If you have to become sensitive to life you must become life, first of all. You look at yourself and see, are you life? In twenty-four hours how many moments are you functioning as a piece of life? Most of the time you are either a thought or an emotion or an idea or an opinion or a philosophy or a belief system or a relationship. Or something like this, isn't it? You are something else. If you want to be sensitive to life, you must be life yourself.

So if you can conduct your body, if you conduct the process of the mind with a little distance, you will naturally become life sensitive. Everything that we have done in the name of yoga is only to bring that life sensitivity because you have to be sensitive to life. Only then you are with reality. Right now you are only ego sensitive. You say, "I am a sensitive person." You have a very big, strong ego: that is what you are saying.

So being sensitive does not mean that for everything you get hurt, angry, or pissed off. This is not being sensitive. If you are life sensitive, you experience every other life as yourself because you are life too. What is sitting around you is as much life as you are. If you sit here as life, intrinsically you know that. If you sit here as a thought, you are completely different from the rest of the existence. If you sit here as an idea, you are completely different. If you sit here as anything other than life, you are fake; you are not a reality. When you are not even reality, when you are not even in touch with the fundamental reality that you are, then everything else is just to be forgotten because it is just a hallucination.

If you want to become life sensitive, a simple process that you do is this: make whatever you think and whatever you feel less important. Try and see for one day. Suddenly you will feel the breeze, the rain, the flowers and the people, everything in a completely different way. Suddenly the life in you becomes much more active and alive for your experience. Then you become life sensitive. Once you are sensitive to this life, there is no way you will not be sensitive to other life. There is no way you cannot be. Because now you will not see "me" as just this body; if you look around, you see that this "me" is all over. Then you are naturally sensitive to everything.

So becoming life sensitive is not an exercise or an ideology or a philosophy. If you are life, you would be sensitive to life. Right now you are trying to be everything other than life; that is the whole problem. You are trying to be a thought, an emotion, an idea, a conclusion, an opinion, a philosophy, an ideology and whatever else. If you just see, whatever your body, mind and emotion are saying is not important, you will suddenly see that you will become extremely sensitive to life.

 "Make everything yours. Why be stingy with your greediness?"

Questioner: You said the spiritual process is about breaking out of the cocoon of demarcated individuality. I have a question related to this: how is it that a six-year-old boy can remember his last life? I heard of one who could tell who he was in an earlier birth, who his parents were and even who killed him, where and how. But after a time, he forgot everything. How is this possible?

Sadhguru: How come he can remember? He should not remember. Nature has given you this cocoon of life so that you do not remember. It has given you a protective wall so that you do not remember, because if you remember you will become a far bigger mess than you are right now. See, with these few years of living here – ten, twenty, thirty, sixty years of living here – people are just struggling with the memories of this life, isn't it? People have great struggles with these few years of memories. Suppose a few lifetimes of memory opened up, you know what a turmoil and struggle it would cause within you? Just being here, you are still struggling with relationships; you are still not able to forget what happened yesterday, what may happen tomorrow. All these struggles are going on.

Let's say you remembered your past lives, and you realized that your dear son happens to be your neighbor's pet dog. Just suppose... (*Laughter*) Because these days, dogs are having a better life than us, yes? (*Laughs*) You know what havoc it would cause in your life and in your neighbor's life? (*Laughs*) And in the dog's life. It would not be good for anybody, isn't it? If you are in such a state of understanding and dispassion that even if you come to know this was your wife, or your mother, or your father, or your dearest friend, you can still continue without even looking at them, then it is okay to know. But if you are somebody who has emotions for everything that you think belongs to you, this is a problem.

People's emotions are only towards those things which they consider to be theirs. Suppose, let's say you have never met your father, or you have not seen your mother, or you had not seen your twin brother or sister in your whole life. Today I show you someone and say, "See, this is your mother." You have never seen her; you have nothing to do with her. But now because somebody told you this is your mother, the moment you see her, suddenly emotions burst forth. From where did those come? You have not built a relationship with this person. You have nothing to do with this person. It is just that when somebody says, "This is your mother," somebody is saying this person belongs to you, isn't it? So, your emotions flare up only in response to those things which you consider to be "mine."

If you have this problem that everything has to be yours, and only then things will happen, then I would say, get a little greedier. Make everything yours. Why be stingy with your greediness? Take it all the way. Make everybody yours; what is the problem? Is somebody there to stop you? (*Laughs*) If that is your way, take it all the way. Or nobody is yours – that is also fine. It is a harder way, but that is also fine. "Nobody is mine" is fine. "Everybody is mine" is fine. "This is mine, and that is not mine" – this is a problem.

So if you remember past lives and you are in this state that, "this is mine, and this is not mine," then you are going to get into lots of trouble. Too much trouble, more than you can handle. If you have reached a point where everything is yours or nothing is yours, then it is okay to remember. Then it would be useful to remember.

So a six-year-old boy, just by chance, remembered something. Sometimes the systems in nature fail, you know. Some data input mistake. (*Laughs*) It happens. It is such a complex structure, so sometimes it happens. It is a little mistake. The necessary protection was not created in a particular child. But even if these children do remember, usually before they grow up, they tend to forget. Lots of children below the age of four clearly remember their past, but by the time they become four years old, it all dies out. After the age of four, they get involved in this life, whatever is around them. Until they are four years old, it is possible, that in their minds the past could be just going on.

I don't know if you are aware of this. In India for a variety of reasons they said this: "Until the child is four years of age, he belongs to God; only after that he belongs to you." They say this because he is full of so many memories, he does not belong to anybody at that time. After that, once his memory goes away, he starts relating to everything around him in a deeper way, and that is when he begins to belong to you. At least, he gives you an illusion that he belongs to you. (*Laughs*) He will break it after some time. Children do, don't they? One way or the other, they do.

So it could happen. It has happened, but generally, such people forget after some time. That capability or that kind of aberration, I would say, happens only at a certain phase of childhood. After that it dies by itself.

> **Questioner:** Does this mean children are naturally spiritual or is this something that has to be cultivated?

Sadhguru: As I said, when a child is born, nature has made a certain level of insurance for him so that he does not turn spiritual too early, because if he does, he will not have the will either in his mind or in his body to carry on. See, the body has its own will that becomes very strong as it matures, especially as it attains puberty and moves on. It is at this time that the will becomes strong. Until then the body does not have so much of a will. You know there is something called an "infant mortality rate"? That is because a very young body does not have that much of a will. So, as I just mentioned, generally up to four years of age it does not have much will. At four years of age, it becomes a little established. From four to fourteen, it has a will; from fourteen onwards, the body has a very strong will of its own.

Mentally also this is true, but physically it is even more so. If a child begins to taste dimensions beyond the physical, then he will have no will to retain the body; the physical body will have no will to sustain itself. It will quit. There have been any number of *bala yogis*, but they never live long. Have you heard of bala yogis? Child yogis? Child yogis never live long. If they survive beyond fifteen years of age, they will pass usually by the time they are twenty-one to twenty-three years old. If they attain when they are a little older, just in the pre-puberty age – let us say between ten to thirteen years – generally by the time they are somewhere between thirty-one to thirty-four, most of them will pass.

Whether you take a Vivekananda or a Shankaracharya[9], any number of people are there in India who passed away at that age between thirty and thirty-four because these are all people who attained at that age. They lived very fiery lives, but they exhausted themselves and they left, because if the body becomes aware before it is established in a certain way, it cannot sustain itself beyond a point. It is not an incomplete life. It is a very complete life. They did more in that short span of life than most people will do in ten lifetimes, even in terms of physical activity. For example, Adi Shankara, by the time he was thirty-two, the things that he did are absolutely incredible. What most human beings cannot do in three, four lifetimes, that much activity he did by the time he was thirty-two, and then he quit. So this is real quitting, where the body has lost the will, and it is quitting.

So are children spiritual? I have said many times, never put children into closed-eye meditations and processes like that. It is simply because of this: if we bring them to a certain dimension of experience when they are very young, we will have very wonderful beings, but we will also bury them very quick.

There was a sage called Krishna Dwaipayana. He was later called Vyasa Muni. Krishna Dwaipayana was born to Parashara, a great sage. This sage Parashara is the one who established hundreds of ashrams around the country because he wanted to establish righteousness and a certain spiritual process everywhere. In those times, there used to be any number of small kingdoms in the subcontinent. He brought many, many

9   Or Adi Shankaracharya: a celebrated ninth century A.D. teacher of
    Advaita Vedanta, and the founder of neo-monastic orders.

kings into the spiritual process because he wanted the political administration to change so that people could benefit. He was a tireless campaigner, but it so happened that some people who were against him attacked the ashram and burned it in the process. He was badly injured in the leg.

So his people, his disciples, put him on a boat and took him to an island where a small tribe of fisher folk lived. Since he was grievously injured, he was nursed by the fisher folk's chief's young daughter. Slowly they got involved, and she bore a child. He was Krishna Dwaipayana. But Parashara recovered, and he left. Those are the times when there is no telegraph or cell phone or anything to communicate. You are gone for many years if you go. When a man went off those days, whether they were kings or sages, when and whether he will come back, you do not know. There is no contact. It is only when somebody else from somewhere comes and tells you some tale that you get news of him – and even so, you don't know how true it is.

So Parashara went away. But the mother went on telling the child what a great man his father was. So the child grew up in great fascination of a father he had not seen. When he was just six years of age he went about telling all the children in the village, "My father knows everything. He knows the sun; he knows the moon; he knows the stars," because Parashara was a great astronomer. "He knows everything. There is nothing that my father does not know." As it is, the man Parashara was beyond one's imagination; he was that kind of a man in his knowing and his wisdom. But in the child's mind, this grew even more. With great fascination, he became one-pointed. He wanted to learn and become like his father. But he was living among the fisher folk; the atmosphere was not conducive for this kind of learning.

So when the child was eight years of age, Parashara once again came visiting. He went by foot, and making a round of the subcontinent took eight years, you know? Today it is different. I go to Delhi today, and tomorrow I am back here. I go to United States, and I am back in fifteen days. But just imagine if we had to walk to Delhi and come back, I would come back after three years! (*Laughs*) So, he came back after eight years – an express trip. There was now no limit to the boy's joy. The father that he had not seen, the man he had visualized and fantasized about as the greatest, had arrived.

Immediately he told his father, "You must teach me everything, everything you know." The father was overjoyed with the boy's eagerness to learn, because where does one find people who want to learn? It is one thing wanting to give; it is another thing to find people who are willing to receive you totally. This boy was showing such eagerness to know. So the few months that he spent there, he started imparting things to him. When the time to leave came and he had to go again, the boy said, "I have to go with you."

Sage Parashara said, "As my son you cannot walk with me. Only my disciples walk with me. My son and my wife cannot walk with me."

The eight-year-old boy said, "Then take me as your disciple. I will cease to be your son right now."

Parashara said, "You are still too young. I will come after a few years. I will take you. Right now it is not necessary."

Now if he makes his round of the subcontinent, even if he makes a super-quick round, it will be at least five or six years. So by that time the boy would be fourteen, and that was his idea. The boy said, "Nothing doing. When you value this knowing, this enlightenment so much, why do you tell me that I must postpone it? I want to go now."

So Parashara looked at the boy not as his son; he just looked at him as a possibility. He saw a great possibility in the boy, and he initiated him into *brahmacharya* or *sanyas*[10].

So the first step of becoming a brahmachari or sanyasi is you have to beg for your own food. Nothing belongs to you

---

10 The path of the divine. A life of asceticism and studentship on the path of spirituality moving towards the highest modifications of the senses.

anymore. So the boy went out begging, and he came back empty-handed. Parashara looked at him, he had an empty bowl. Initially he thought, "Did he eat it up and come? Is he taking such liberties because he is my son?" Then he saw the boy's face. He had not eaten. The whole day he had been out, but he had come with an empty bowl.

So he asked, "What happened?"

The boy said, 'Wherever I went, because of this sacred ash, because I am wearing the clothes of a sanyasi, because my mother is the daughter of the chief here and because I am your son, people are filling my bowl with food. I don't know if they would do that for other sanyasis. Because of my parentage and lineage, wherever I go people are filling my bowl. But I see there are so many other children who are still hungry on the street. So I gave the food to them. I begged more and more, and then I gave it away."

Then the father saw, "Okay, I have more on my hands than I thought." He said, "So what are you going to do about your food?"

The boy said, "It does not matter. I take this vow in my life that unless everybody around me has eaten, I will never eat." He kept this up all his life. They say he lived for over 340 years. These 340 years, he kept up this vow that he took at the age of eight: that "unless everybody around has eaten, I will not eat."

So this boy was initiated into sanyas, but still he lived that long because the first thing that Parashara did was put him on very severe yogic practices to make the body resilient beyond normal limitations. Then he was initiated into various other processes. So unless things are done like that, initiating very young children would mean physically shortening their life.

So are children spiritual? A child is generally less messed up, less concretized, less set. That makes him more of a possibility. At the same time, because a child's perception is taking in much more than your perception is taking in right now, he is both a plus and a minus. A child is drinking up life much faster than you are because everything is new and fresh for him. So this is a tremendous possibility if he is given the right kind of atmosphere. In time this is a terrible problem if the wrong types of things are around him because without any discretion he drinks up everything.

So is a child a better possibility than an adult? In some ways, yes. But a child is probably looking forward so much to doing all the stupid things that the adults are doing. He is yet to see that it is not worthwhile. Most adults have not yet seen it is not worthwhile, isn't it? So a child is yet to see. That is also a disadvantage. Over four years of age, he is so eager to do everything that the adults are doing that he wants to grow up fast and be like somebody else.

But this can be set right by creating the right kind of ambience of life around him. The same trees, the same plants, the same flowering and the same flowers and same fruits, depending upon the atmosphere and the ambience in which they grow, they produce different levels of fragrance and different levels of sweetness, isn't it? The same seed, but still it is different, depending upon what we create around it.

 "That is the reason why you dig your own well – so that you have water throughout the year."

Questioner: You say that when a person is blissful, he becomes more malleable, more free, less burdened by individuality. What exactly is this bliss? Can you describe true bliss, Sadhguru?

Sadhguru: (*Laughs*) How can I tell you? This question may actually spring from a certain misunderstanding about the nature of bliss. See, today even psychedelic drugs are being named "Bliss." If you say "bliss" in the West, they will think you are talking about a particular tablet, a particular drug.

There is no such thing as "true bliss" and "false bliss." When you are in truth, you will be in bliss. When you are really in touch with truth, you will naturally be in bliss. So being blissful and not being blissful is like a litmus test for you to see whether you are in truth or not in truth. Probably this question is coming from a certain mindset: "If I am just watching the sunset, if I become blissful, is that true bliss? Or when I am saying my prayers, if I become blissful, is that true bliss? Or when I am meditating and become blissful, is that true bliss?"

Most people misunderstand pleasure as bliss. You can never sustain pleasure. It always falls short of you, but blissfulness means a state that is not dependent upon anything. Pleasure is always dependent upon something or somebody. Blissfulness is not dependent upon anything. It is of your own nature; once you are in touch with it, you are in it, that's all. Blissfulness is not something that you earn from outside; it is something that you dig deep into yourself and find. It is like digging a well. If you open your mouth and wait for the raindrops to fall into your mouth, when it is raining, a few of them may get inside. But still it is quite frustrating to quench your thirst by opening your mouth to the rain. Besides, the rain is not going to last forever. An hour, or two, or three, it lasts, and then it is over.

That is the reason why you dig your own well – so that you have water throughout the year. So whatever you are referring to as "true bliss" is just this: you have dug your own well into yourself and you have found water that sustains you all the time. It is not something that you open your mouth to when it rains. No, all the time you have water with you. That is bliss.

 "Yogis are not against pleasure. It is just that they are unwilling to settle for little pleasures. They are greedy."

Questioner: I have heard of the moon being symbolically invoked in mystical literature, but is there any real connection between the moon and mysticism?

Sadhguru: The moon and mysticism are deeply linked. Should we wait for the moon to come out before we talk about it? But it does not matter whether you see it or not; it is there, anyway! It hasn't gone.

There were two morons. One of them said, "For a vacation let's go to the sun." The other said, "Maybe it will be too hot out there." But this one said, "Oh, we'll go at night!" (*Laughter*) Just because your perception is limited, nothing has changed. Even on a new moon day the moon is still on, isn't it? Actually, the influence and impact of the moon is much stronger on the day when you cannot see it than on the day you can.

So what does the barren surface of the moon have to do with mysticism? The very process of human birth, the body-making process, is very deeply connected with the cycles of the moon. As you know, the fundamental reproductive process in a woman is very much linked to the cycles of the moon. So the timing with which the moon goes around the planet and the cycles that human beings go through within themselves and the process of creating this body, are very deeply connected.

As one shifts from the calculations of the logical mind to intuitive ways of looking at life, the moon becomes more and more important. This is because as you dig deeper into yourself to know life, the connection between the moon and the making of this body becomes more and more apparent. Different positions of the moon have different kinds of impact on human physiology and the human mental make-up. So a part of the dimension that is beyond the logical has always been connected to the moon. There are many things happening between the full moon and the new moon, and again, between the new and full moon. How every day, the different positions of the moon can be made use of for human well-being, is a well-established part of Indian culture. The moon is a reflection. A human being or human perception is also a reflection. Any perception is actually a reflection. As reflection is the nature of the moon as we know it, the deeper perceptions of life, which cannot be explained logically, have always been symbolized by the moon.

Now something related to the moon, in English, is referred to as "lunar." Do you know the next step? Lunatic! The moon has been linked to madness because outside Indian culture, any kind of illogical behavior has always been termed madness. But here the illogical has always been accepted. Here, we called the moon "*soma.*" Soma means intoxication. There is a difference between intoxication and insanity, isn't it? Nobody seeks insanity, but people do seek intoxication.

People seek intoxication because they do not know how to put down the terrible logic of their mind which is going on breaking the world into pieces. You may not be getting along with anybody in your life, but with your drinking buddies you are real close. That is because people who sit and drink together, somewhere they have found a little bit of oneness. Their logic and their resistance have melted down, and they have laughed together, they have sung songs together, maybe cried together, maybe rolled in the gutter together. (*Laughter*) They have done things that they would not otherwise do. Someone who cannot even sing in the bathroom starts singing and dancing in the street because the intoxication has loosened him up a little bit. So that is the essence of intoxication and that is the attraction of intoxication.

So the moon is referred to as "soma," which means the source of intoxication. If you have gone out somewhere on a moonlit night where there are no electric lights, or if you just look at the moonlight, slowly you will get lightheaded. Have you noticed this? If you do certain things to imbibe the moonlight into you, you will get really drunk. Just with the moonlight. This is not logical. We can do it without the moonlight also, but moonlight does it very well! So it is because of this quality that the moon is referred to as "soma," the source of intoxication.

Now the science of yoga gives this pleasure to you to be internally drunk all the time. See, yogis are not against pleasure. It is just that they are unwilling to settle for little pleasures. They are greedy. They know if you drink a glass of wine it just gets you a little buzz and again nothing, and tomorrow morning, headache and the works. They are not willing to settle for that. Now, with yoga, they can be all the time totally pissed drunk, but hundred percent stable and alert. To enjoy the intoxication you must be alert, isn't it? If you drink, you try to stay awake and enjoy the intoxication. And that is how yogis are: totally drunk, but fully alert. This cannot happen by drinking something or taking in a chemical. Nature has given you this possibility.

There has been a lot of research in the last couple of decades. It is said that a particular scientist from Israel went to great lengths researching, for almost thirty years. What he found is that in the human brain there are millions of cannabis receptors. The only logical explanation they could give for this was, sometime in history the whole of humanity was smoking marijuana, which, of course, is not true. So why are there so many millions of cannabis receptors in every brain? It is simply because if you keep your body in a certain way, the body will produce its own narcotic, and the brain is waiting to receive it. After years of focused research, this scientist said that it is only because the human body is producing its own narcotic that feelings of peace, pleasure and joy can happen within you (without any stimulus from outside). It is the chemistry of your joy or your blissfulness.

So this scientist wanted to give this chemical, naturally-produced in the body, a name. Normally people call their discoveries by their own names, but he wanted to find an appropriate name. So he went through various scriptures around the world. He could not find anything that he was satisfied with. Then he came down to India and he found the word "*Ananda*," or bliss. So he called it "Anandamide." If you generate sufficient amount of Anandamide in your system, then all the time you are drunk, but fully awake, wide awake.

I want you to know that instead of spending twenty years of research, if you had just asked me, I would have had you stoned without anything from the outside! Yes, I can have you completely drunk without any external input, with simple yoga. If you just sit here, I will have you completely drunk – intoxicated, but fully aware.

The reason why we are against alcohol and drugs is because it intoxicates and takes away your awareness and spoils your health and destroys you. Suppose these drugs were such that they intoxicated you, but they also made you very alert and intelligent and had a very wonderful impact on your health, then all of us would be into them. Isn't it so? So Shiva, the first yogi, is a great yogi who sits in great alertness; at the same time, he is a drunkard and a smoker of pot. He is intoxicated all the time, but at the same time fully aware and alert.

Every yogi is working towards this. Because, if you do not know the intoxication of the divine within you and if you do not know the alertness of the mind, you will completely miss life. The only way to perceive life at its best is when you are intense and absolutely relaxed at the same time. Right now the problem with most people is if you ask them to be intense, they will become tense. If you ask them to relax, they will become lax. (*Laughter*) Both in laxity and tension you will miss life. Now to be intense and absolutely relaxed – this is only possible if you are absolutely aware, and at the same time, you are absolutely drunk.

So this means you are producing your own narcotic and consuming your own narcotic, and it has a tremendous impact on your health, well-being, mental alertness, perception, everything. So are you the ball and the bat and the catcher also? Yes, that is because that is how your system is made. That is how the atomic is made; it is self-contained. That is also how the subatomic is made. That is how the individual is made. That is how the cosmos is made.

As I said earlier, this blissful state is not a goal by itself. This blissful state will eliminate the fear of suffering. Only when the fear of suffering is gone, only when this anxiety of "what will happen to me," is completely eliminated from you, will you dare to explore life. Otherwise you only want to protect it. It does not matter where you go, if you are not in that blissful state, security becomes the only issue, doesn't it?

Let's look at it: why did you go through the process of education? It is in search of security. Whether a career or a business, it is all about security. Marriage is about security. Everything is about security: physical security, emotional security, psychological security, social security, financial security, any number of varieties. But it is all about security.

As long as the fear of suffering is constantly playing its role, you will not dare to really go into the deeper dimensions of life. Only if you are drunk like this – totally pissed within you, but fully alert – there is no fear of suffering. Now you are willing to go anywhere. Wherever the hell you go, what does it matter? If they ask you to go to hell, you will go there, because you have no fear of suffering. Only when you are in that state of intoxication are you willing to explore life.

 "When you become absent, your presence is tremendous. When you try to be present, you have no presence at all."

Questioner: You talked of the moon as a source of intoxication. Traditionally, Indian spirituality has attached a great deal of significance to the phases of the moon, hasn't it? What exactly is the significance of Pournami (the full moon) and Amavasya (the no-moon)?

Sadhguru: You tell me. Between a Pournami night and another night, is there no difference? There is lots of difference, isn't it? Ask the people who are a little mad. They know the difference very well! What is important now is, why have people who are a little mad turned even madder?

Now take the volume of this microphone as an example. Suddenly the volume is increased and it starts blaring. The talk is the same, but suddenly it is a little louder and clearer. It is just like this. There was a little madness; you gave it a little extra energy or you increased the flow of energy, and now everything seems to be magnified. It is the same with love, with laughter, with joy, with everything. It is just that on the full moon day the energy is a little higher.

What makes the energy a little higher? For one, there is a certain aesthetic quality about it. Anything that you look at, if it is beautiful, your receptivity to that object suddenly becomes greater, doesn't it? Anything that you consider ugly, the moment you look at it, your receptivity to that just comes down. So one thing is that the full moon has a certain aesthetic quality; this definitely improves your receptivity.

Another thing is that the planet has moved into a certain position in relation with the satellite that makes the vibrations very direct and forceful. You know the tides are rising, because the gravitational pull of the moon is working on the water more than on other days. So water is spilling over and trying to jump up. Similarly your blood is trying to jump up. When the circulation of blood increases in your brain, whatever is your quality gets enhanced. If you are little mad, you become madder. If you are peaceful, you become more peaceful. If you are joyous, you become more joyous. Whatever is your quality, it is just being pushed up. People only noticed madness, because most of the people are in that state, okay? But it is not only madness; it is so about everything on a full moon night. If you are a very loving person, on Pournami your love will overflow.

Now what about Amavasya? What is the difference between Pournami and Amavasya? There is a lot of difference in the quality of meditation on Pournami and Amavasya. For a meditative person, Pournami is better. But Amavasya is a good day to do certain rituals and processes. On Amavasya nights, your energies are supposed to be roguish. Like a rogue elephant, your energies run amok. That is why Amavasya nights are used by tantrics[11]. It gets the energies moving. Pournami nights have a more subdued quality, which is more subtle, pleasant and beautiful – more like love. Amavasya is a baser energy. If you want to compare the two, you can say Amavasya is more sex-oriented and Pournami is more love-oriented. Amavasya has a grosser nature and is more powerful. Pournami has a subtler nature. You cannot feel the power, it is so subtle. The kundalini behaves in the same way: on Pournami days, it moves very gently and on Amavasya days, it moves in great bursts and thrusts. There is more violence about it on Amavasya.

Pournami is a tremendous presence. The presence of the moon is so clear that wherever you look, everything becomes translucent, doesn't it? The vibration and the light have that quality where everything gains a new kind of aura. The vibration and feel of the full moon is very different from the moon in other states. And the magnetic pull is also different. The *Ida*[12] and *Pingala*[13] within you also function in a different way. The *prana,* or vital energy, flows in a different way. The blood flows in a different way. Your whole energy flows in a different way because the vibrations have changed.

It is not that you cannot remain in Pournami every day. You can. If you have some mastery over your sun and moon, you can remain in Pournami even in hot sunlight. It is possible. When you do certain kriyas, there is coolness in sunlight; even on a hot day there is the beauty of Pournami within you. If you have a certain mastery and control over this, you can choose to have Pournami every day. Or you can choose Amavasya every

---

11 Practitioner of tantra: the science of using mantra, the sound and yantra, the form. Refers to an esoteric Indian spiritual tradition.
12 One of the three major pranic channels in the human body. Located on the left side of the body, it is feminine (intuitive) in nature.
13 One of the major pranic channels of the body. Located on the right side of the body, is masculine in nature.

day. Or you don't choose at all: whatever is happening in
nature, you can just enjoy all the stages of life as they are.

Pournami is a tremendous presence and Amavasya is an
absence. A logical mind always thinks that presence is powerful
and absence means nothing. But it is not so. As light has power,
the absence of light – or darkness – has its own power. In fact,
it is more overpowering than light, isn't it? Night is more
overpowering than day because darkness is just absence. It is
wrong to say that darkness exists; it is just that light is absent
and that absence has an overpowering presence. The same can
happen here. Whatever Gautama could do when he was with
his body, he could do a million-fold more when he left his body.
That is why dissolving the body is known as *mahasamadhi* or
mahaparinirvana. It is because absence is greater than the
presence. When you dissolve, you become a tremendous
presence. Even in your own consciousness, right now, when you
become meditative, it means you have become absent. When
you become absent, your presence is tremendous. When you try
to be present, you have no presence at all. An ego has no
presence. But when you become absent, there is tremendous
presence. The same is true with Amavasya. Gradually, the
moon has disappeared, and that absence has created a certain
power. This is why Amavasya is held as important.

For a hardworking, tough, aggressive person, Amavasya is
definitely an important aspect. For a person who is very
sensitive and subtle, Pournami is a very important aspect. Both
have their own power. In terms of qualities, Pournami is love,
and Amavasya is aggression. But we can make use of both.
Both are energy. The processes we do on Pournami and the
processes we do on Amavasya are very different.

Gautama chose Pournami for his enlightenment. Buddha
Pournami is a very significant day for every person making an
attempt to walk the spiritual path. On this day, some 2,500
years ago, something very tremendous happened. After that,
the world has never remained the same. In his own silent way,
Gautama changed the world forever. Into the whole aspect of

man's aspiration and seeking, he brought a different quality. That man's flowering 2,500 years ago has made a significant change for spiritual seekers all over the world. A person seeking to grow on the spiritual path cannot ignore Gautama. Gautama flowered on a Pournami because for a person on the path of effortlessness, Pournami is best. For the practice of Samyama[14], Pournami is definitely best. But if you are doing hard sadhana[15], like mantra, japa[16], and tapa[17], Amavasya is best.

 "...Bhuta Shuddhi is a basic sadhana in yoga to transcend the limitations of the physical and to become available to a dimension beyond the physical."

Questioner: Can you tell us something about the Pancha Bhuta Aradhana[18] process that takes place at the Dhyanalinga temple? I understand it is about balancing the five elements. How do people who attend benefit from it?

Sadhguru: Shivaratri, the darkest night of the twenty-eight day lunar cycle, is a significant day in terms of what happens in the different strata of the planet. It is not just about the darkness of the night. Generally, in the tradition it is said that the planet,

---

14 An eight-day advanced residential program conducted in Isha, where participants maintain absolute silence while experiencing explosive states of meditativeness, and receive a powerful practice.

15 Spiritual practices which are used as a means to realization.

16 A spiritual practice in which a mantra is uttered (aloud or within one's mind) in repetition, usually for a specific number of times.

17 Lit. heat. A preparatory spiritual practice to heat up or intensify one's life energy in order to experience long periods of meditativeness and higher dimensions of perception.

18 An offering of the five elements to the Dhyanalinga on the 14th day of the lunar month. Participants can attain physical and mental well-being by purifying the five elements constituting the body.

Mother Earth, broods on this night. On this night she does not sleep. Or in other words, the activity of the five elements in the planet is much more intense, in a way.

The five elements need to be constantly integrated. The very forces of life – the dynamics of the movement of the planet and other forces of life – are constantly trying to dismantle the integrity of the five elements as a combination of creation. So it is on this night that Mother Earth tries to integrate herself, or tries to bring these five elements together in a much more forceful way than on other nights.

Usually the Amavasya, the new moon night, lasts for thirty to thirty-two hours in this period, and the intensity of the elemental activity is much greater. It has been noticed that if you germinate a seed in certain controlled conditions on different days of the lunar month, on this day the germination slows down. The very way the plant grows slows down because the elements are busy maintaining themselves. They do not contribute as much to the growth of the plant because the soil, like the whole planet, is trying to integrate itself on this day.

This is a fantastic natural process happening on the planet, and this is also a fantastic opportunity for one who is aware to use this as a way to integrate the five elements in his system. How these five elements behave within you will determine just about everything. "Bhuta" means elements; "bhuta shuddhi" means to become free from the taint of the elements; it means to become free from the physical. So bhuta shuddhi is a basic sadhana in yoga to transcend the limitations of the physical and to become available to a dimension beyond the physical.

Shiva, who is referred to as Bhuteshvara, attained what is called "*bhuta siddhi*," that is complete mastery over the five elements. Anyone who has attained to bhuta siddhi can, for instance, dematerialize his own body. There are yogis who go into a room, locked from outside, and when someone opens the door, nothing is there, not a trace of that person. That is, you don't find his body, you don't find his ashes; you don't find anything. He is simply gone because he dematerializes his own physical system. Someone with bhuta siddhi, or mastery over the five elements, can not only integrate, he can also disintegrate his own system.

It recently happened that someone who had a Linga Bhairavi Yantra[19] in their home found lots of water upon and around the yantra. This was kept in a place where there was no room for any kind of water to enter. It is just that one life which did not belong to that family made use of this energy to completely dematerialize and disappear; all that was left was a little pool of water.

You can even dematerialize that water, so that not a drop is left. Somebody did the job a little inefficiently! So the body and everything was gone, just a little pool of water was left. If you weigh fifty kilograms – or let's talk realistically; if you weigh a hundred kilograms (*Laughter*) – anywhere between seventy to seventy-two kilos is just water. So he did not leave seventy kilos or liters of water. Either he was a small person or part of the water was dematerialized and part was left.

So this family could not believe where this water came from, and they were saying, "A miracle has happened..." I said, "Shut up and clean up the place." (*Laughs*) Nobody takes note of the fantastic miracle that is happening every day in the making of the body. The air that you breathe is becoming body, isn't it, in many ways? The water that you drink is becoming body. But nobody takes note of such a miracle. A pool of water around the Bhairavi Yantra, that is a miracle for them. I said, "Take note of the real miracle that is happening every day. If you miss this miracle, you will never get to know what that miracle is."

So during Amavasya, especially at the Pancha Bhuta Aradhana in the Dhyanalinga temple, a powerful possibility is created for the whole month (not just for that day), where you can integrate your system and enable the five elements in your body

19   A unique and powerful energy form designed and consecrated by Sadhguru to bring prosperity and well-being in all aspects of one's life.

to bind much better. "Isn't it doing well right now?" you might ask. From one body to another, there is a very big difference as to how these five elements are integrated. How well integrated determines a lot of things about that person, almost everything, I would say. And if this body has to become a foundation, a stepping stone to a bigger possibility, not a hurdle, it is very important the system is properly integrated. If the bhuta shuddhi, which is the basic form of yogic practice, is done properly and the elements are sufficiently purified, then the binding becomes better.

Being in the Dhyanalinga temple does a phenomenal job of integrating the system, not just on the surface level. Health does not mean, "Oh, my pulse rate is okay, my blood pressure is okay, my sugar levels are okay." That is only a consequence. The real thing is whether the five elements are well integrated and functioning in perfect cohesion within the system. Then there is just no need for anybody to worry about what the medical diagnosis is saying because if the elements are functioning well and are strongly integrated, health just happens by itself.

If you learn to integrate it consciously, we could also some day, when it is needed, teach you to disintegrate it, so that you will save us the bother of burial or cremation! You will save some labor – and that is good, you know? (*Laughs*)

 "I am stoned all the time, but fully conscious."

Questioner: You talk about space and time being an illusion and about bursting the bubble of one's individuality. How did that happen to you? How did you go beyond the bubble of space and time, Sadhguru?

Sadhguru: As I said, both space and time are a creation of your conscious mind. If you transcend the limitations of your conscious mind, there is no such thing as space and time. Modern physics is talking about eleven different dimensions in the same space. Yoga has always talked about twenty-one different dimensions in the same space.

Time and space are both stretchable. You can alter them whichever way you want. You can make what is a 1000 light years away alive right here. You can make 10,000 years ago, or what will be 10,000 years later, right now; because here and now is all there is. So according to science (I am not talking mysticism here), everybody knows time and space are big illusions. You can make whatever you want out of them. You may have seen this in your meditations. In one session you sit, and that hour-long session looks like eternity. Another session, when you just settle down into a certain inner situation, you close your eyes, you open your eyes, and they are already saying, "Break." (*Laughter*) This is because both time and space are stretchable.

Your question is about how it happened to me. Many years ago, on a certain afternoon, I happened to be sitting on a small hillock, which I loved, which I knew very intimately. (*Laughs*) Until that moment, I always thought "this is me" and "that is the other." I handled the "other" quite well, but still "this" was "me," and "that" was the "other." Until then I also managed my time and space very well. (*Laughs*)

On that particular afternoon, suddenly I burst forth into an experience: I did not know which was me, and which was not me. What was me was all over the place. The very rock that I was sitting on, the very air that I was breathing, the atmosphere around me, everything became me. That does not make logical sense, because as I said before, if you want to make any kind of logical sense, you need two. Without two, there is no logic. But suddenly there was no two; it was all me. Everything was just me.

I thought this lasted for about ten to fifteen minutes, but when I came back to my normal senses, about four-and-half hours had passed. I was sitting there with my eyes open, fully conscious. I was not in any kind of trance; I was fully conscious. But time had just flipped, and I found for the first time in my adult life, tears flowing down my face. Before then me and tears were impossible. I had always been peaceful and happy; that was never an issue. But here my shirt was wet with tears and I was bursting with a completely different kind of ecstasy, which the body could not contain. When I really shook myself back to my normal senses and tried to understand what was happening to me, the only thing that my mind could say was that maybe I was losing my balance; maybe I was just going off my head. But it was so beautiful that I did not want to lose it for a moment.

The next time this happened to me, I was sitting with my family at the dinner table. Actually in my experience, it was just two minutes, but seven hours had passed. This started happening regularly, and one day I just sat down, and I thought it was maybe twenty, twenty-five minutes, but thirteen days had passed. I was sitting right there, eyes open, fully conscious. It never occurred to me that I should eat or sleep or anything. I sat in one place for thirteen days, not with any effort, not with any intention, not with any attitude towards attainment or anything; I simply sat down and when I looked around again, thirteen days had passed.

So after that experience I had on Chamundi Hill, time and space just started flipping in me. Suddenly what was there was here; what was then was now. I could see everyone's past, present and future at the same time. It was all one grand confusion. But it was also utterly beautiful. I realized then that all human experience is self-created. Though most human beings believe that their experience is created by events around them, I realized that it is hundred percent self-created. You can make your experience whichever way you want. Just to feel a moment of pleasantness within himself, how much indignity each human being is going through. Just to experience one moment of completeness, what a circus people are making of their lives. And it will never be enough. There will always be a longing in human beings for something more. This compulsion to go beyond compulsion is a fundamental human need.

So time and space are very much the creation of your logical mind. Once you transcend that, there is no time and space. If you know life, if you know the truth, you know how everything works. If you want love or ecstasy or bliss, it is yours. The deepest human desire is freedom. And that is available too.

But you do not even have to cross time and space to be blissful. Blissfulness will happen to you in so many ways. Right now I think there are lots of people here who are practicing Shambhavi Mahamudra[20]. You sit down in the morning, and in twenty-one minutes you become totally blissful; drunk but fully aware.

Look into my eyes and see: I am stoned all the time, but fully conscious. This moment, if I want, I can flip; or this moment, if I want, I can be alert and conduct the situation the way I want. As I said, Shiva, the first yogi, was inebriated all the time. At the same time he was a perfect ascetic – sitting there in absolute meditation and drunk at the same time. This is what it means. And this is how all of us should be – absolutely inebriated, but perfectly stable within ourselves. Now the need for seeking something outside will completely disappear. Once you are blissful by your own nature, your life becomes an expression of your blissfulness, not a pursuit of happiness. And that is the shift that needs to happen in every life.

---

20 A powerful yogic practice of great antiquity, imparted in the Isha Inner Engineering program.

CHAPTER 3

THE BIG BANG – OR ROAR?
Where Physics Meets Metaphysics

"The more you unravel the scientific process,
the more mysterious this world becomes."

"If you look inward, a different dimension opens up. Now instead of things getting more complex, you get to clarity."

Sadhguru: The biggest problem is the moment you say "spirituality," somebody starts talking about God, someone else about mukti, someone else about nirvana and someone else about the Ultimate. They are all already up there. You cannot do anything with people who are already up there. If somebody is down here, you can do something with them. You can only take a step if your feet are on the ground, isn't it? The moment you talk about God, you are not here anymore; you know it all. You can only start a journey from where you are. You cannot start a journey from where you are not. If you are willing to come down to where you are, then we can see what the next step is. If you are already on the third step to heaven, what can I do with you?

In pursuit of knowing that which is not known, science has gone in one direction. As it progresses, its intention is to convert everything into knowledge. Everything that is not known, we want to cull it down into that which is known. So in the last 100 or 150 years, a phenomenal effort has been made by the scientific community. We have invented various instruments that are like third eyes, enabling us to see things that we could not see. Whether it is a microscope or a telescope, these are all the third eyes of science. They assist you in seeing that which you could not otherwise see. But by seeing microscopic life and by viewing the stars and galaxies, nothing significant has been known. Life has become more mysterious than ever before.

If you look up at the sky at night, how many stars do you see? Have you ever counted them? Did you make an attempt to do so? When I was young, I made a serious attempt to count, and I counted somewhere around 17 – 18,000 stars, and then it got all mixed up. But I thought there must be another 8000 or more stars. We can probably see 10 – 15,000 stars with our naked eyes. But today we have powerful telescopes through which we can see over two billion stars. And yet, has the world become less mysterious or more mysterious? More and more mysterious, isn't it? The more you unravel the scientific process, the more mysterious this world becomes.

If you looked at a leaf a hundred years ago, it was just a leaf. Now it is not just a leaf. We know billions of things that are happening in it right now, and we still do not know the leaf. We are not able to figure out a single leaf in this whole existence. This planet is full of trees – I am sorry, it is not a planet "full" – there are very few trees left actually! (*Laughs*) But with whatever the number of trees we have left, still we do not know a single leaf.

So this method of arriving at knowledge – trying to know life by ripping it open, trying to know life by dissecting it – has not worked, because the more we look, it is only getting more complicated. If there was no technological offshoot to science, no technological benefit coming out of it, science would have been dismissed as a totally nonsensical effort. Today most people in the world do not know what science is. They only know technology, because they are enjoying technology. Technology is just an offshoot of science, a consequence of it, but it is not science.

Actually, a mystic has no issues with science. Science is not different from a spiritual process; I am talking about fundamental science. His issue is with technology, because a lot of technology is simply plainly destructive. Trying to do everything that we can do in this world is a very foolish way of doing things. The development of technology has been in many ways most unscientific.

So if we come to science as such, essentially I see it as a thirst or a longing to know the nature of the existence, which is not in any way different from the spiritual seeking. It is just the approach and the methodologies employed which are different, but essentially both of them want to know the nature of the existence.

See, when we say a "spiritual seeker," unfortunately most people assume that he is God-oriented. A spiritual seeker is not God-oriented; if Devil is the chief of existence, he wants to know that. We want to know what is true; we are not interested in proving our belief systems, because we don't have any.

So, through my perception, what I see with the scientific community is that their longing to know is fine, but somehow, they have crippled themselves by believing that everything that they want to know will happen through physical means. I feel this is the main crippling factor in the development of science.

When we talk of "exploring the mystical," we are not trying to dig into creation, because if you dig into creation, it will only get more complex. It will not bring clarity; it will only bring more complexity. That is why the yogis looked in a different direction. We looked inward. If you look inward, a different dimension opens up. Now instead of things getting more complex, you get to clarity. It is because of this that we say that those who look inward have a third eye. They see things that others cannot see. They have brought a new clarity to life.

So this is the fundamental nature of yoga and of mysticism: only if you become absolute non-existence, you will know existence. If you go looking around in the existence, you will not even know a leaf of a tree. If you study the leaf of the tree for the rest of your life or the next million years, you will still not know it absolutely. So the only way is, if you become non-existence, the nature of existence will become apparent to you. The whole point of mysticism is to sink into this one (*referring to oneself*) because this is creation.

Knowing creation within you makes a wonderful difference for you. Knowing it within you gives you an enormous amount of freedom to use your life in ways that you have not imagined; to use these life energies in ways you never thought possible.

Recently, I happened to be in a presentation by a popular scientist[21]. He has written a book called *The Endless Universe*. It has become very popular in the scientific circles. So he called this particular session "Beyond Big Bang," because until recently the scientific community believed that everything has happened because of the Big Bang. But now they are saying, "It was not just one; many bangs must have happened." It has been held that some billions of years ago, this particular Bang happened, which has resulted in all these planets and this universe. But now they are saying this Bang is not the only one.

I will not go into the whole science of it, but it was amusing for me because these theories are beginning to sound just like yogic lore. This is something that we have always known from within. But slowly they are not only beginning to talk like yogic lore, they are beginning to describe the same forms and shapes that we have always held as sacred and have always worshipped.

As I said, in the yogic system, we do not believe that you can ever go out into the existence and find out everything that is there – a belief which scientists have also come to. When the scientist says it is an endless universe, he is obviously saying you can never find out what it is. You can never travel from end to end and say, "Okay, this is existence." We recognize that

---

21 Referring to Paul J. Steinhardt and/or Neil Turok, distinguished
     theoretical physicists and authors of *Endless Universe*.

this is an ever-expanding universe; there is no way to travel from one end to the other and know it, because by the time you travel across, it would have expanded. For everything in this universe, the basic law is that anything that travels at the speed of light will become light. Suppose I move this finger back and forth, it is fine. But if I make it go at the speed of light, this finger will not remain physical; it will become light. Light is the only physical aspect that can remain; everything else will disappear. Because of this we can only travel at most a kilometer below the speed of light; that is the top speed you can attain. So if you travel at a speed below the speed of light, by the time you go from one end of the universe to the other, it would have grown much faster; there is no way you can ever travel the whole distance. That is the reason why we are saying it is an endless universe; we can never travel to the end. This is something that has been said thousands of years ago. Since it is an endless growth, it is ever-expanding. Now the scientists call the universe endless. In yoga, we have always said it is ever-expanding.

And so, the best way to know this existence is by turning inward. Whatever has happened in the existence, all of it is in some way recorded in this mini-universe, in this body. It is because of this recording, because of this reflection of the existence, that we said that the human being is created in the image of God. So this expression that was uttered way back, thousands of years ago, in the yogic realm, has found reflection in every religion in a misinterpreted way. We just said, "Everything that happened in existence has happened in a small way here inside you." If you know this one (*pointing to himself*), you know everything that is happening out there. This human being is just a reflection of the whole creation. We cannot separate the creation and the Creator. So in the same image as the creation is the Creator. When I refer to the Creator, I am not talking about God having the same features as me. He may be like me, but definitely not like you, because you have all cut off your hair! (*Laughs*) There is a possibility that he looks like me, but definitely not like you.

So, I will make what science is trying to say today very simple. I think recently certain scientists from a Scottish university were saying that there is a link between what we call "dark matter" and "dark energy." You know, these days, scientists are saying everything comes from dark matter; everything in this existence is dark matter. And now they have started talking about dark energy. They thought these things were separate. Now they are saying that they are linked.

Let me tell you how yoga explains creation from within. This is a dialectical culture. I can make it all ABC if you want, but let's enjoy the culture. There is a certain beauty to the terminology. Because it is speaking about a dimension which is not in our logical perception, it is best to speak in dialectical ways. The story goes like this: Shiva is sleeping. When we say "Shiva" here, we are not talking about a person or the yogi that I mentioned before. "Shiva" here refers to "that which is not"; that which is nascent. "That which is not" can only sleep. And he has always been referred to as the "Dark One."

So as Shiva sleeps, Shakti comes looking for him. She wants him to come awake because she wants to dance with him; she wants to play with him; she wants to woo him. Initially, he does not wake up. After some time, he does. Anybody who is in deep slumber, if you wake him up, he will get a little angry. If you were in deep sleep and somebody came and nudged you, it would not matter how beautiful that person was, you would get angry. (*Laughs*) Isn't it so? So he gets angry, roars and rises. That is why his first form and his first name is Rudra. The word "Rudra" means one who roars.

I asked the scientist, "If there is a series of Bangs, could it be a roar?" If it was a "Bangbangbangbang" rather than "Bang-bang-bang-bang," it becomes a roar, like an internal combustion engine. So I asked this scientist, "Was it just one bang or was it a continuous thing?" He thought about it, and then he said, "It cannot be just one; it must have been longer than just one moment." And I said "Why are you calling it a Bang? It is a Roar, isn't it?" So Shiva roared and stood up.

Now, this scientist had put up a picture of the first form that came up when the Big Bang happened. It was like a tower coming up, with a small mushroom spread out on the top. This is exactly the form the yogic culture has always described. It is because of this dialecticism that they said that he woke up and became ready for creation. So they described him as the phallus. Because we are human beings, we think that the creation of life means sexuality, and there is body involved in that process. So we say the first roaring form that he took was that of a phallus.

Now, wherever there is a vacuum state, there are some particles called virtual protons and virtual neutrons. Through them, creation is happening and disappearing randomly. It is based on this that the Quantum Theory has propounded that creation is, at random, happening and disappearing. But, according to modern science, if you take any vacuum state and apply a little bit of electromagnetic energy from outside, all these random happenings will now find a proper defined role. They will all start moving in elliptical orbits. These are the fundamentals on which the whole theory of Quantum Mechanics has grown.

So when Shiva was awakened by Shakti, he roared, rose and then he cooled slowly. He was a Rudra for some time. When his anger cooled, he became an ellipsoid. Today scientists are saying that the first form was an ellipsoid; the whole universe was in the form of an ellipsoid, or what we call the "linga" – the first form. This ellipsoidal form was just one large mass of gases, still roaring. But gradually it cooled. When Shiva saw Shakti, we say he got up because he was enamored by her. This is how he took on a form of linga. Then slowly, because she wooed him continuously, he cooled down. This cooling is what has caused creation, according to science. These hot gases cooled and became masses of creation; the whole universe is just that. So here we have both the dark matter and the dark energy: Shiva is referred to as the "Dark One," and the first form of Shakti, or dark energy, is called "Kali."

So this universe is contained in an ellipsoidal form, depending upon the heat, the expansion and contraction of gases, and the density of their mass. Most of it is empty. Here and there, mass particles, stars and planets and everything else happened. This, in our perception, is phenomenal, but in reality if you look at it, most of it is still unformed; very small particles of creation have happened. The rest is all just emptiness. If you look up at the sky, there are just a few spots of creation. The rest of it is all vast emptiness, isn't it?

Now, as I said before, what is being perceived now in a phenomenally roundabout way was perceived a long time ago. It is true within every human being if you look deep enough. Today, we know from our experience, that there are a 114 chakras or energy centers in the body. The basic bio-energy system, which we refer to as "prana," has 114 junction points or important meeting-places. There are 72,000 *nadis,* or pathways or channels. If you cut this body, you will not see them, but as you become more and more aware of the movement of energy you will see energy is not moving at random, but it is moving in particular patterns. The energy moves through 72,000 patterns or channels, and these meet at 114 points in the body. One hundred and twelve are within the physical body, two are outside the body. This manifestation itself is a representation of the cosmic-scape.

Out of these 114, eighty-four are of a certain nature. The remaining are of a different nature. The first eighty-four belong to the past; the rest belong to the future. We say Shiva roared eighty-four times; that means eighty-four Big Bangs have happened and eighty-four universes were created. Slowly, over a period of time, these universes lost their form and kept spreading away, became lighter and then disintegrated.

Now, if you just focus on certain parts of your body (I shouldn't be saying this because you may start imagining all kinds of things!), you might notice that there are three dimensions to your forehead. The right side is known as Rudra, the left is known as Hara and the middle is known as

Sadashiva. These three dimensions are a revelation of how existence has happened. This is why we said the third eye is between the eyebrows. Everything that you want to know about the existence is revealed just by being here. These are the three dimensions or stages of the development of existence. Creation went from a primordial state to a roaring state, then to a settled state, and then to a transcendent state – all these three dimensions have manifested themselves in the physiology in a certain way.

So we are saying eighty-four Big Bangs have happened until now, and only a total of a 112 can happen. Another two are non-physical. Creation happened, expanded to its limits, obliterated itself and again started over. The lifespan of this universe, in which we exist right now, is about eighty-four billion years. Right now, scientists say this universe is about 13.6 billion years old. So it is a very young universe. If you are going to live for eighty-four billion years, 13.6 is young, isn't it?

So this physical body has happened in the same way that this whole creation has happened. Today you know that if you cut a tree (please don't do such things!), there are rings in a tree which will tell you almost everything that has happened on this planet for as long as the tree has been here. Similarly, if you look into this body – you don't have to even cut it open – it tells you how the whole of creation has happened.

So this is the eighty-fourth cycle. And this will continue to happen till it reaches 112. These 112 universes will be physical in nature; the last two will be perpetual universes. That is, after the 112th, the next time creation will happen in a semi-physical condition, not in a physical condition. That will be 113. After that, the 114th is a completely non-physical creation, a no-thing, which is right now un-manifest. A no-thing will manifest itself, in the subtlest possible way, and this will live maybe hundred times or thousand times more than the physical, but still not forever. It will live for an extraordinarily long period of time. After that we don't know what is next. We

generally think everything will be obliterated after that. That is
what yoga says. Eighty-four times Shiva has roared. He will
roar 112 times; after that he will not roar any more. He will
step out; that means the nothingness itself will be a universe. It
will not be physical existence.

There are various other aspects connected with this body. And
the way cosmology has developed, all these could have been
perceived just by looking inward. We have spent I don't know
how much money, time, energy trying to explore these things.
But if you are willing to look in – just for a moment, if
you simply look in – it is possible for every human being to see
this.

So, based on this, because you live and exist in the eighty-
fourth universe and you have eighty-four chakras of a certain
nature, yoga developed eighty-four basic *asanas*, or postures.
There are 112 different types of meditation, but eighty-four
basic asanas, because these eighty-four relate to past memory.
The rest is the future. This past memory has to be released. The
information or the karmic bondage goes back as far as these
eighty-four Big Bangs do. So everything is recorded in this
body, and that is why physical nature is the bondage.

This is how stable your body is. At the same time, see how
fragile it is. If the next inhalation doesn't happen, you are gone,
isn't it? We are so fragile, but at the same time, see how sturdy
we are. Look at all the things that human beings can do and
have done. How many things we have overcome, how many
things we have accomplished on this planet. (*Snaps his fingers*)
It will all be gone like that someday. At the same time, the
things that man can do are remarkable and unbelievable in
their own way.

 "*The Indian temple was never created as a place
of prayer.*"

Questioner: I have been to many powerful places, such as Kailash and Manasarovar, and have had very intense experiences. I have equally intense experiences at the Dhyanalinga. Could you explain a little bit more about the Dhyanalinga, Sadhguru?

Sadhguru: As I said before, the first form that creation takes on is that of an ellipsoid. Today, it is common knowledge in cosmology that the core of every galaxy is an ellipsoid. It is from this core that the galaxies are spinning out. And from our experience we clearly know this: if you take your life energies to a certain level of intensity then the final form that your life energies take is that of an ellipsoid. Before dissolution happens, it will take the form of an ellipsoid. So from this we know that the first form and the final form are both ellipsoids. Before creation, it is un-manifest; when creation begins to happen, it becomes an ellipsoid, and then everything else happens. When it begins to dissolve, the final form that it takes is that of an ellipsoid. After that, there is dissolution. So the first and the final form being an ellipsoid, this form is seen as a doorway to the beyond. It is both the front door and the back door.

So linga-making became a very deep science in the Indian subcontinent. It is not just here. Almost everywhere in the world there are lingas. In Africa, there are a variety of terracotta lingas which are used for occult purposes. The Native Americans in South America have used lingas for similar purposes in a different context. In Europe there used to be many lingas before the Inquisition. One which has survived is in Greece. It is known as the "Navel of the Earth." This was consecrated about four thousand years ago by Indian yogis, and it is one that is still maintained, but now they have moved it from its original place to a museum.

Some of the African lingas are in American museums today. What used to be established in a certain type of temple, people dug these out and took them to their museums, because they found them interesting and thought they were phallic symbols.

These are very powerful forms which are created with a definite purpose. There are varieties of lingas, created for a whole variety of purposes.

The Dhyanalinga is unique because it has all the seven chakras established in it. If you look at it one way, it is like a live being, the highest possible human being, the most intense possible human being, without a physical body. The energy body of a person has been created; or in yoga, we would say, he is like Shiva, the highest possible intensity. If you go anywhere beyond that, it will be dissolution. So the Dhyanalinga is in that kind of a state. It has the energy body of the highest possible being.

This may be too weird for you, but actually, in theory, it is possible for us to create a physical body for him. Practically, there are too many difficulties, but in theory, it is possible. He has the energy foundation. If we want, we can add flesh and blood to him. But then what is the point? If he gets flesh and blood, we have to share our food with him. Then he will get up and go to the toilet. Then he will sleep. He is better this way! He has no physical body, but he has an energy body of tremendous vibration.

In the seven days of the week, you will notice that every day the quality is different. Essentially, the Dhyanalinga was created to initiate people large-scale into meditative processes. People who do not know anything about meditation come and sit there. They thought they would sit there for five-ten minutes, and they simply sit there for an hour or two, because the very reverberation takes you into meditativeness, without a single instruction. Without any kind of instruction, without any kind of preparation, it makes a person meditative. When we first opened the temple, there was lots of resistance in society because it is a temple without any rituals. There are no rituals here, no offerings, no mantras. It is in total silence because it does not need any of that.

When you consecrate a certain space, if you consecrate it through mantras and certain other processes, it needs regular maintenance. If you do not maintain it, it becomes a withdrawing force which is very damaging for people. They have told you that if you keep an idol at home, it must be maintained on a daily basis. If you do not do this, it can become harmful. They are saying this because if you create a form of a certain vibrancy and if you do not maintain it at that vibrancy, it becomes a withdrawing force. If you are in that space where a form is withdrawing in a powerful way, it can cause more damage to you than it could help you.

Many temples, unfortunately, are moving in this direction because people do not know how to manage them. The necessary discipline to manage them is disappearing in most of the places. You need to understand, the Indian temple was never created as a place of prayer. It was not a religious place. Only in the last 600 – 800 years, the temple is being turned into a religious place. Otherwise it was never so. Temples were created as energy centers.

Now if your problem is fear, you go to one kind of temple. You have no love in your life: you go to another kind of temple. You need prosperity: you go to another kind of temple. Like this, different energy centers were created. Maybe in northern India this aspect is less obvious, because most of the ancient temples in this part of the country, which were created in a scientific way, have gone long ago in the invasions. Now there are only the *bhakti* movement[22] temples here. If you come to the south, the traditions are very much alive. For people who come from southern India, there is a clear instruction right from their childhood. When you went to the temple, nobody told you to pray to God, to give an advance check for what he is going to give you later, or anything like this. They told you, if you go there, you must sit there for a while.

The science of temple-making in India took a big beating when the bhakti movement happened, about eleven to twelve hundred years ago. A *bhakta* or a devotee does not care for

---

22 Referring to a time in India when devotion became prevalent, and devotees built temples out of the strength of their emotion, rather than the science of temple-making.

science. For him his whole growth depends on the strength of his emotion. Devotees are given to exaggeration. That is natural for them, so it is okay. A devotee can exaggerate as much as he wants about his deity, about his guru. He can exaggerate because he is trying to grow through the single process of his emotion. Emotion will not flow without exaggeration. If you love somebody, you have to make up all kinds of things about that person. Otherwise your emotions will not continuously flow. If you logically look at it, you will ask yourself, "Is she okay? Is she not okay? This is all right about her, but this is not all right about her." So the love affair is finished. You have to see, "Oh, she is fantastic!" (*Laughter*) Only then it flows. So devotees are allowed to exaggerate as much as they wish. Nobody should stop them, because that is their process. When you are trying to reach the Ultimate through your emotion, if you curtail the exaggeration, emotion will dry up, and it will not work.

All the ancient temples were consecrated by the yogis, but in those 300 – 400 years that the bhakti movement swept the country in a big way, the devotees built temples. Anybody who had a piece of stone and a chisel built one temple. That is why you see, in the middle of the street, on the median, on the side, everywhere, there is a temple. These shrines were built by devotees. They wanted to put them up everywhere.

The Dhyanalinga is a combined possibility; all the seven dimensions are there in it. Because all the seven chakras are fully active, it is oriented towards meditativeness. But the other aspects are very much there. It is unique, because all the other lingas are generally consecrated towards one direction, in one particular dimension. Only in a few places there are lingas which carry two or three chakras in them. There have been a few attempts where they have tried all the seven. There used to be about three of them in the present state of Bihar, but they are all gone. They were razed to the ground a long time ago. Their energy forms still exist, but there is no physical presence anymore. Towns have been built over them. We have located more than half a dozen of them which people attempted to create in the past. They reached certain levels, but they were not completed. So right now there is only one linga like this where all the seven dimensions are included in one form. That is what makes the Dhyanalinga very unique. And this temple is always in silence with no rituals because it does not need any maintenance.

One great temple in the south which is incredibly beautiful, architecturally, is the Thanjavur temple. It is believed to be made up of about 130,000 tons of granite. The sixty meter high *vimana*, or tower, is the tallest in south India. When they built it eleven hundred years ago, there were no cranes, no trucks, so they built a ramp which is over six kilometers long, and they slowly moved the dome up.

The linga itself is some twelve feet in height and twenty-five feet in circumference. And this stone came from Saurashtra in Gujarat. They wanted the stone from the banks of Narmada. I want you to just imagine, over a thousand years ago, transporting a close-to-300 ton stone from Gujarat to Tamil Nadu. No highways, no trucks, no cranes. You can imagine what it takes. These were a completely different kind of people; they were not thinking about their well-being at all. I do not know how many thousands must have died just transporting that stone from there to here.

A particular yogi was the architect for the temple and also the one to consecrate the temple; he was known as Karuvurar. There is a temple in honor of him in another town in Tamil Nadu. He was an accomplished yogi. It was his idea to build this, and the king financed this idea. But as the temple was being constructed, because it was a project of many years, some problem arose. The king's ego got a little trampled, and so the yogi left. But he could not really leave the project, so he put up a small hut on the southern side of the temple.

The moment you put your hut on the southern side it means you are clearly indicating that things are not going well here. So the yogi just camped there, and they went about constructing the temple. Then when they had to put the linga into what is known as the "*Gauripeetam*[23]" ("*avudaiyar*" in Tamil), whatever they did, they could not get it in. Clueless as to what to do, they came to the yogi and asked him, "What shall we do? It is not going in." So the yogi took his spittoon, spat into it – he was chewing *paan*[24] – and said, "Take this, put it inside, and then place the linga; it will go in." They did as he said, and it did go in. He was a great devotee and spitting on the linga is something impossible for him, but he did this just to indicate it was destroyed. It was already gone. There was nothing left there.

So this is a very powerful linga in a withdrawing sense. It can cause lots of damage to people's lives. Especially for women it could be very damaging and disturbing because it works in their system in a different way. Tamil Nadu politicians are aware of this. None of the Tamil Nadu politicians ever visit the Thanjavur temple, because if they go there, there is a firm belief that they will lose in the elections. You want to send someone there? (*Laughter*)

Right now the temple is under the authority of the Archeological Survey of India. They once came and asked me a few things about the temple. I told them, "You leave the temple in my hands for two weeks. I will kill the linga, because there is no way to revive it. If I kill it at least it will be a good monument." But they cannot make such decisions, you know? So, it is still like that. For over a thousand years, it has been withdrawing, not dying. They have always told you, if an idol is even slightly damaged, take it and put it in a well or a river where people cannot access it, because it becomes a withdrawing force.

Coming back to Dhyanalinga, its uniqueness is that it does not need maintenance. If nobody enters this temple for a thousand years, it will still remain the same. It does not need anybody's

---

23 The base or the feminine portion of a Linga.
24 Rolled or wrapped betel leaves usually containing a mixture of areca nuts, tobacco and slaked lime paste. Traditionally it is chewed to cleanse the palate and for improved digestion.

care. Another unique aspect of the temple is that fifteen days in a month, from one phase of the moon to the next, men maintain the temple. In the other phase of the moon, women maintain the temple. There was a lot of social resistance at one point. "How can women take care of the temple? Have you checked whether they have their periods or not?" You know, there was this kind of nonsense going on in the society around us. But now all that has settled.

In a month's time, approximately 1 – 1.25 lakh people visit the temple. There are all kinds of people; there is no religious divide. A number of Muslim and Christian families come regularly to the temple because they experience it in a certain way, and they are not required to change their beliefs. It is a yogic temple. It is geared towards one's spiritual evolution.

Another basic reason why it was created is this: to do sadhana by yourself and to do sadhana in the intimacy of a guru's presence is very different. Usually only a few people could do the latter because of various limitations. Now everybody has the opportunity to do their sadhana in the intimacy of a guru's presence, and that too a guru who does not have the problems of a physical body. He is much better, you know? I am on about twenty hours; for four hours when I sleep, I am down. But he is on twenty-four hours. It's good. (*Laughs*)

 "Peace is the last thing I'm seeking. You 'rest in peace.' This is the time to live."

Questioner: I wonder if you could explain a little more about the consecration procedure at Mahima[25]. Would you tell us more about that process? I saw a lot of ingredients went into that pit, but I really didn't understand what was happening.

---

25 A 39,000 sq. ft. dome-shaped meditation hall, the largest of its kind in the Western hemisphere, consecrated by Sadhguru. Located at the Isha Institute of Inner-Sciences, Tennessee, USA.

Sadhguru: It looked like we were making *sambar*[26]. (*Laughter*)

Questioner: I really don't know how you consecrated it. What were the steps that you followed? That's a big subject, I suppose, but I really would like to know now that I have attended the consecration.

Sadhguru: See, this is always happening in the world – constantly, all around us, one substance is being made into another. This transformation is happening all the time. If you make mud into food, that is called agriculture. If you make food into a human being, this is called digestion. If you make a human being into a mud again, we call this cremation. (*Laughter*) If you transform the physical into the non-physical, that is called consecration. Why the need to transform the physical into the non-physical? Because that is your longing. When you say "I want to walk the spiritual path" what you are saying is "I want to touch something which is not physical." It is just that the word "spirit" is so terribly corrupted. If you leave the social implications of the word aside, essentially, when you say "spirit" what you are saying is you want to touch something which is not physical, something spiritual.

You know, today we can take an egg from a woman's ovary and a sperm from a man, and in a laboratory we can put it in a conical flask (not a test tube... I think it's too narrow). (*Laughter*) If you create the right kind of condition, you could come out of a conical flask. (*Laughter*) It is possible. We are close to that. It is very much possible. When there are so many women or when there are so many wombs, I don't see why there is all this effort to make babies in a conical flask. It doesn't make sense to me; it is just such a wasteful effort. So what you call a womb is, essentially, a conducive atmosphere to create a life, to nurture a life for a certain period of time.

---

26 A popular South Indian stew made with vegetables and lentils.

In case you slipped out of your mother's womb too early, then we put you in an incubator, because the normal atmosphere would be too much of a challenge for a child who came out a little too quick. Have you been to that ward where the prematurely born are placed? So here you find all these babies which are born a little early for some reason; babies with mothers who are in a hurry... (*Laughter*) When I was in Mumbai they took me once into this neonatal ward. There were about twenty-six children in this, and they were in different states of incubation. It was quite amazing how these creatures survived because they are not fully done, you know. Maybe a hundred years ago, all these babies would have died. Natural selection would have happened. Now, because of medical care and support, they are slowly nurturing all these babies into normal life. I think only about fifty to sixty percent of them could become normal; others would always be not quite normal right through their life, because certain things did not happen for them in a protected atmosphere. They came out too soon.

All of you are like that. (*Laughter*) Physically, you are fully developed. If only there could also be an incubation to make you fully evolved, spiritually, before you pop out of the womb all this would not be necessary, you know. If somehow we could make future pregnancies last for eighteen months...! If we could make all the women so meditative that they could hold on to their fetuses longer, nurture them to a certain level of spiritual blossoming and then let them out, then we would not need Mahima. Because Mahima is just a womb or an incubator for neonatal care! (*Laughter*) All those premature babies that came out, this is just to nurture them to a different level of blossoming within themselves.

So this transformation from one dimension to another is always happening, whether a flower blossoms, or a fruit ripens, or a sprout comes out of the earth. One thing is becoming something else. One substance is becoming something totally different. The flower and the mud: aren't they the same substance essentially? But look at the difference. So, using all the same ingredients largely, we make something else out of them. The womb is one kind of incubator; the fetus is also another kind of incubator. You, as a body, are also another kind of incubator which is nurturing something else within. A fetus, or the formation of this bundle of cells in the mother's womb, by itself is not life. The womb created the fetus; the fetus became a receptacle for life, and nurtured that life which is still continuing to happen.

Somebody in their garden produced a thousand roses out of their plant. Someone else has just managed one in ten years. It depends on what kind of soil, what kind of care, what kind of nourishment went into this. Similarly, everybody has the same kind of body: one person can make this into so many things; another person struggles with it; another person is somewhere in between. Each person is in his own way.

Unfortunately, too much nonsense has been said about the systems of yoga and *tantra* and the essential nature of the spiritual process. So, the moment I say "spirituality," people say "I want to be peaceful." If you want to be peaceful, you must be dead. (*Laughter*) You don't walk the spiritual path for peace. I know worldwide this kind of nonsense is happening. To be peaceful you don't have to be on the spiritual path. A drink will do it. If you go climb one mountain and sit there, it will happen. If you take a long walk and lie down, you will sleep peacefully. You have a full stomach, you will sleep peacefully. (*Laughter*) It is a shame that so-called spiritual teachers are going about telling people that this is about being peaceful. The longing for peace has essentially come from troubled minds, minds that are torturing themselves. For them, peace is a big commodity that they have to seek. If you are not using your mind for self-torture, why would you think of peace? Would you seek the exuberance of life or would you seek peace? Only if you have become an expert in self-torture, peace seems to be the greatest thing. A bullet in your head does it very well actually. (*Laughter*) It renders you peaceful instantly.

About four months ago, someone came to me and said, "Sadhguru, your face is so peaceful..." "What! Me and peaceful? Look at my eyes and see: I'm like a bloody volcano!" Don't insult me by saying I am peaceful. (*Laughter*) Peace is the last thing I am seeking. I mean it. You *rest* in peace. (*Laughter*) This is the time to live. For people who have lost control over their mental faculty, what should have been a miracle has become a misery-manufacturing machine for them. So this spiritual process is not about being peaceful.

I met a group of people in Israel recently. When I said "*Namaste*," they said "*Shalom*." I asked them, "What does shalom mean?" They said, "This is the highest form of greeting anybody. This means peace." Then I said, "Why would peace be the highest form of greeting another human being?" That would be so only if you happen to live in a troubled region. Peace is not the highest form of greeting for me. If you are steeped in violence, peace is the highest longing that you can have. In rural India, particularly in south India, if you go into the village, they will not ask you how you are; they will just say, "Have you eaten?" That is the only greeting, because if you have eaten what else can be wrong with your life? The rest is only your mental nonsense, isn't it?

So in a society where people are constantly struggling for survival, asking whether you have eaten is the highest greeting. In a society where they are steeped in violence, peace is the highest greeting. In a society where they are deprived of love and care, "I love you," is the highest greeting. When I come to the United States people come up and say, "Sadhguru, I want my hug! I want my hug!" (*Laughter*) So somewhere people are in some kind of downtrodden condition where compassion is the highest greeting. But these are all social realities which can change.

So once these needs are fulfilled, nobody is going to value these things. If you are well-fed, peaceful, blissful, happy, well-loved, with nothing to complain about, you will not value food, peace, love, compassion so much. The spiritual process is not about this. As I repeatedly keep saying, the spiritual process is about removing the foundations of the physical so that a dimension beyond the physical becomes the main force in your life. Being peaceful, being loving, being compassionate, being gentle, being kind, being pleasant to each other is just civility. Anybody with a little sense understands that if you don't maintain a pleasant demeanor in the world, everybody else will give you double unpleasantness for the unpleasantness that you share with them. It is just simple sense. Unfortunately, most of the time in spiritual processes is wasted in inculcating these qualities because most people have not even learned that it is a sensible thing to be pleasant.

In terms of experience, we want to make this (*referring to the self*) very pleasant. We want this to be blissful, ecstatic. But, as I said before, even being ecstatic is not a goal by itself. If you are blissful by your own nature, then the important thing is that you are no more the issue. There are other issues in this existence; we can look at those. But if you are an issue, what other issue will you take in your hands? You will not touch anything. When I am enough trouble myself, why do I want to take on this one or that one? When I am no more an issue, now I am willing to dig into the whole existence and see what it is all about.

So mysticism evolved only in those places where people learned the technology of being ecstatic by their own nature. For you to experience a little bit of pleasantness within you, if you have to drink, if you have to dance, if you have to do some other crazy thing, then you will never explore any other dimension of life. Keeping yourself pleasant itself is a great challenge, and it is a fulltime job. Isn't it so? The pursuit of happiness has become the goal of life itself. Happiness is not the Z of life. It is the A of life. It is not the end-product of life. It is not something that you achieve. It is something that you start with. That is the square one of life. As children we all started joyfully.

Only if you are blissful you will truly explore all aspects of life. Otherwise you will not dare to. If maintaining a little bit of pleasantness within you is such a big challenge, where is the question of taking on bigger challenges?

There was a time when we believed that whether the tree in your house bears fruit or not depended on God's will. But we took charge of these things. Now if this is not bearing fruit, we know what the problem with it is and what to do with it. All these things we slowly figured out. So, if this one (*referring to the self*) has not blossomed, it only means we are not doing something right with it. It is as simple as that. When we understand that, that is when a spiritual process actually begins.

So, when you are not an issue, when being peaceful or joyful or blissful is not an effort anymore, then naturally you want to know what is behind everything. It is not an induced quest. It is very natural for human intelligence to look for it. You cannot help it. The spiritual process is not a conscious choice; it is a kind of compulsive behavior. (*Laughs*) But unless you handle it consciously it will not yield. That is why it looks like a trick. Longing for the boundless is compulsive, but unless you become conscious, it will never work.

If you are stuck to the rigid formats of your logical mind, it looks like an impossibility. It looks like there is no way. If you come to India, you will see this: people will go to, let's say, a Devi temple, bow down to her, chant all the mantras, the prayers. They are saying, "You are everything." Then they go to a Ganapati temple, bow down to him, chant all the prayers, everything. They are telling him, "You are everything." Then they go to the Lakshmi temple; they do the same. They go to the Vishnu temple; they do the same. To Shiva, of course, they say, "You are everything." Because when you say "you are everything," you are saying "you are the center of the universe." And it is true. The cosmos does not have a fixed axis. You can make anything the very center of the universe. It is all in your consciousness. So these people move seamlessly from one thing to another; they just don't have a problem with anything. And if you want to access other dimensions of life, if you want to know, experience and handle other dimensions of life, it is very important that you have no rigid structures in your mind.

So, coming back to your question, consecration is just this: you are making one thing into another thing. What is just a physical thing you are making a god out of it; you are making it the very center of everything. People keep asking me "Sadhguru, are you going to make another Dhyanalinga in the United States?" I tell them "No use. And there is no need to because you can bring that here whenever you want." Dhyanalinga does not belong to time and space. If you are willing, it is here also. We can establish one space where we won't consecrate anything, but if all of you are willing, that will become the Dhyanalinga temple.

Now, I am beginning to talk mumbo-jumbo (*Laughter*) because life is mumbo – and it is jumbo. (*Laughter*) It is big. The biggest thing in existence is life itself, isn't it? The biggest thing in the existence is not some god sitting somewhere. The very life process itself contains the creation and the Creator. If you are willing to go beyond the surface substance of the self, suddenly everything is plastic. You can move one thing to another, another thing to another. It is all mixed up. As I said before, time and space are stretchable; you can make them small, you can make them big, you can make them anything you want. So the consecration process is touching the borders of that.

I don't want to ask questions which will make some people go into flights of imagination, and make others feel depressed that they can't feel anything. All this is not necessary. But if you came into this hall the day before the consecration and the day after, you might have noticed that there is a big difference in the way the space is. If you meditated here yesterday and if you do it now, you will notice a big difference in the way it happens. So, you change the quality of the space simply because you change the reverberations.

This is why always yogis and mystics chose spaces which are small and generally deep into the earth. Caves are just cubicles in the earth. The mountains and the caves are always popular with spiritual people because they want to be surrounded by earth. They don't want to be in a wide open space where they can't retain the energy. Those mystics who were further evolved in these aspects went into subterranean spaces. In your perception, this could be just as big as a mustard seed. But for them, it could be a whole city. There are lots of people living there and doing their sadhana. They are living a full-scale life. In your perception of space, it may be like a grain of sand. In their perception and in their life experience, it is big. You can stretch space like this.

 "Everywhere else people believe God is the Creator and you are a piece of creation. This is the only culture where we know that we can create a god."

Questioner: I have heard that there is a tradition of animal sacrifice in the Kali temple at Dakshineswar. They say that this happened even when Ramakrishna Paramahamsa[27] was alive. Somehow I can't help wondering how an enlightened being like him could allow it. Would you ever allow such a thing, Sadhguru?

Sadhguru: I thought you would leave me alone at least! (*Laughs*) So the question is, "Oh, someone like Ramakrishna, how could he kill an animal?" Ramakrishna always talked about loving every creature in existence. Whenever such teachings are given, people take these teachings literally, by the word, not by what it really means. One of the devotees was really struggling with this. If I tell you "you must love everybody," that is going to be a struggle, isn't it? Immediately

---

27   A mid-nineteenth century spiritual master who lived mostly in Kolkata. A devotee of Goddess Kali, he frequently went into ecstatic states of samadhi.

your boss, your mother-in-law and all those people will come to your mind. (*Laughter*) How to love all of them? "Yes, I am willing to love everybody except these two people. If you exclude those two people, I am willing to love the whole world." (*Laughter*)

Once it happened: a mother and her seven-year-old boy went to the cemetery. This is the first foray the boy had made into a place like this. The mother was dedicated to a particular grave, where she would often go and sit. The boy was interested in the whole cemetery, so he went from tombstone to tombstone, reading the inscriptions. He went on a whole tour of the cemetery, came back to his mother and said, "Mom, every tombstone says: This is the most wonderful man that ever lived. So where do they bury all the horrible people?" (*Laughter*) Dead people are always wonderful, isn't it? It is only the living who are trouble. The dead are great, aren't they? That is why we worship them! We never worship them when they are alive. The moment they die we worship them, because we like the dead.

So, since Ramakrishna went on preaching, "You must love everybody and everything, not just your neighbor," I want you to know what this "everything" means. (*Laughs*) Jesus was very kind. He just said, "Love your neighbor." At least with Jesus you can move into the right kind of home! (*Laughter*) But Ramakrishna is cruel. He is telling you, you must love everybody and everything -- every creature on the planet.

So, one devotee was really getting messed up by this because his bed was hugely infested with bedbugs. They were giving him hell, but he could not kill them, because the guru says you must love all creatures. And a large part of the bedbug is human, you know? He has a tank full of humanity in him, isn't it? (*Laughter*) So this devotee was going through hell, not killing a single bug. He could not bear it anymore, because many nights passed without sleep.

One morning, totally sleepless, he walked to Ramakrishna's house. He wanted to ask him, "Can I kill the damn bugs at least?" So as he entered Ramakrishna's house. He saw Ramakrishna sitting in the yard, with a mat which had bugs in it. And he was very methodically killing each of them one by one, one by one. The man saw this and thought, "Okay, you can kill bugs, but lovingly." (*Laughter*)

So, why did Ramakrishna allow animal sacrifice in Dakshineswar? Because Kali likes it. Ramakrishna never ate meat, but Kali likes animal sacrifice. Whatever she likes, he does. Why does Kali like it? You need to understand what these deities are about. Indian culture is the only culture where there is a technology to make gods. Everywhere else people believe god is the Creator and you are a piece of creation. This is the only culture where we know that we can create a god. We have a whole technology of how to create one. We never saw god as Creator; we only saw what you call "god" as an ultimate flowering which every human being can reach.

It is a completely different way of looking at life, a completely different dimension of understanding and knowing. These – forms for example, Kali, a fierce form – were created by human beings. We created various types of gods and goddesses. Some are very fierce, some are pleasant, some are horrible, some are very loving, some are fearful. There are various types for different purposes. We created certain energy forms and consecrated them. And we created certain sounds and attached processes to keep them alive and to keep them going.

So, Kali needs sacrifice. If you do not perform sacrifices, she will slowly die. If she dies, Ramakrishna cannot live, because his whole spiritual process is based on Kali. If she dies, the whole possibility is gone for him. So he will allow anything to keep that going.

Let's understand first of all what this sacrifice actually means. I want you to look at this from a proper perspective. I am not speaking in favor of sacrifice, okay? (*Laughs*) You know all over the world at one time or the other, the sacrifice of animals, and even humans, has existed. In just every part of the world, it has been there. When people want to sacrifice something, they

always pick an animal or any life form which is in a vibrant life
state. Nobody ever sacrifices an old man, isn't it? When they
want to do a sacrifice, whether it is a chicken or a goat or
whatever, it must be vibrant young life, in just the beginning of
its youth. That is the kind they choose. They also know a
whole procedure for creating a certain atmosphere and
suddenly breaking the body. Once the body is broken, the life
will burst out. They have a method of how to use this life
towards some other goal. So some of these deities were made
like this.

In a Kali temple, if you give up the sacrifice, it means you have
decided you do not want Kali, because she will die over a
period of time. She will become a receding force for some time,
and then she will die. That is how she is made. Her very
creation has happened out of this kind of process.
Understanding this, Ramakrishna allowed it to happen. Even
now it is happening. In most of the Kali temples, there is a
sacrifice every day.

Is it cruel? Anyway, you eat the meat, right? A butcher will do
it somewhere else. Instead, they are using the life energy in the
temple in a certain way. In any case, the goddess does not eat it;
it is people who eat it in the end. So seeing this and
understanding this, Ramakrishna allowed it to happen. Instead
of slaughtering the animal in a slaughterhouse, you use the life
energy also in a particular way to enhance the deity that you
have created.

Would I allow sacrifice? Yes, but not animal sacrifice or human
sacrifice. But without throwing out some kind of life energy,
you cannot do anything. You will just end up talking
spirituality. Right now, generally what is happening in the name
of spirituality is that somebody has read a book, and if you sit
there in front of them, they will vomit it on you. They are
articulate all right. They read lots of books. But what they are
vomiting on you is not about life; it is about a book. However
sacred the book is, it does not matter. I am not saying this with
any disrespect to the book. With all due respect to all the books

on the planet, the fact is they were written by human beings. Maybe they were spoken by God himself, but still they were written by human beings.

Right now whatever I have spoken here, if I ask all of you to sit down and write it down, you will see, there will be 300 different versions of what happened today. That is because the human mind is given to enormous distortion. You say something to somebody today about something that you witnessed; that someone else expresses it to someone else. Suppose it went through twenty-five people within twenty-four hours and then came back to you. Do you think you will even recognize the story? Human minds are given to distortion, and most of the time this distortion is not intentional. The mind always functions from its identifications, so naturally it distorts things.

So if you want to know anything, the best thing is to read this book (*referring to the self*). This book was written by the Creator himself, no question about it. In this there cannot be any distortion. So yoga decided, no books; you just read this book. We do not trust anybody else's book. It does not matter whether my father or my grandfather or my guru wrote it; we do not trust anybody, because everybody is capable of distortion. But this book is constantly being written by the Creator himself. In this there is no distortion. So you look at this one.

When they talked about sacrifice, they trusted nothing else other than life. Now, this sacrifice has taken on many forms. There have been some extreme forms where people have sacrificed their own children. There have been people who have sacrificed themselves. In the tantric way of life, people have sacrificed themselves. And there have been temples – I do not want to name them right now – where instead of using animal sacrifice or human sacrifice, they used something else. It is something unthinkable for you because it is supposed to be a sacred place. They have used the menstrual fluids of a woman, because that is also life. Instead of killing a baby, they just used the menstrual blood, because it is life-making material. With that they created whatever you refer to as "gods."

I am also constantly making a sacrifice even though we are not slaughtering anybody or anything. Now, if you do not throw some life into something, nothing happens. (*Claps his hands*) That is a sacrifice. If you don't throw out some life, nothing will happen. We can demonstrate to you what this sacrifice can do (*referring to the clap*). It can just blow you up because it is just life energy being thrown. So without throwing out some life – whether you do it by cutting an animal or a human being or using menstrual fluids or this (*claps again*) – you cannot do anything worthwhile. You can only talk. Talking spirituality is just entertainment. It does not take you anywhere. It psychologically satisfies you; maybe it brings solace. If you are seeking solace, all you are seeking is bad psychiatry. In the name of spirituality, what is generally offered is just uneducated psychiatry. People are trying to fix people's minds. That is not what a spiritual process is about. That is not what mysticism is about. Mysticism is about transcending the limitations of the physical to explore a dimension which is both beyond the physical and which is, at the same time, the basis of the physical. That which is the basis of the physical is the Creator.

When we say Creator, how did this idea come to us first of all? You crawled out of your mother's womb and saw so much creation. Obviously, you did not create it. So you looked at your mother and thought, "Oh, she doesn't look like a person who can deliver the planet." Okay, she delivered you, but not the planet. You looked at your father; he also does not look like that. You looked all around; nobody looked like that. So you concluded that there must be somebody up there. It is a very simple childlike conclusion.

Some religions on the planet believe God is up there. Some religions believe God is down there, in the core of the earth. Those religions which see that God is in the planet, somewhere deep inside, they walk a little more gently upon this planet. Those who believe God is up there, they walk aggressively, because this planet is not so valuable to them. They think they are going to heaven anyway. If you are so dead sure that you are going to heaven, I do not see why you are waiting and what you are waiting for. You must take the opportunity today, isn't it? The problem is, to a point where it is convenient, you believe just about anything. But if I ask you, "Anyway you will go to heaven; why don't you jump into the pond and drown yourself right now?" Then your answer is no. But anyway you will go and land in God's lap; why postpone it even by a day?

It is just that we are unwilling to see that we do not know a damn thing about life. It does not matter how much you have heard, how much you have read, how many discourses you have attended, still you do not know a damn thing about life. You do not know where you came from, where you will go. There are just stories. Now even if the stories that you have heard are true stories, as far as you are concerned they are just stories, isn't it? You can entertain yourself with a story. You can give solace to yourself with a story. But you cannot liberate yourself with a story.

Let's come back to this idea of sacrifice. Actually even in your life, if anything significant has to happen, you have to sacrifice something. Otherwise the result won't happen. You have to throw life into something; only then it happens. If you are successful in your business, in your career, you know you threw your life into it. Are you not sacrificing your life eight hours a day in the office? Is that not a sacrifice of life? To build your business, to build your career, to bring up your children, are you not sacrificing your life? You are. Even to go to college are you not sacrificing your life? Life is somewhere else on the street, but you go sit in the college and study those damn books, don't you?

Once a kindergarten teacher was in an inspired state. She had just taught the children how Isaac Newton got knocked by an apple and came to realize gravity. She got a little poetic, and she told the kids, "How wonderful it must have been! Just imagine it: Newton just sitting there under the tree in a garden, an apple

falling and he suddenly understanding that apples fall down."
Now the kids always knew that apples fall down. So when she
said this, one of the little boys stood up and said, "Yes, but if
we sit in the school and go on reading these books none of
those wonderful things will happen." (*Laughs*)

 *"...if I have the necessary support, I can pull out a
Devi from every tree, every flower, every human
being..."*

Questioner: How was the Linga Bhairavi[28] consecration
different from the Dhyanalinga consecration in your
personal experience? Is birthing a goddess less demanding, less challenging?

Sadhguru: As I have said before, there is going to be only one
Dhyanalinga Temple, but I am willing to do any number of
Devi temples.

But first, I notice a certain inflection in the question: "Is the
Devi any less than the Dhyanalinga? Is the feminine form less
than the masculine?" No, but the feminine form is definitely
less than a combination of the two and that which is beyond.
The Dhyanalinga is not a representation of masculine form;
there is both the masculine and feminine sitting there – just in
case you missed it till now, being a woman. (*Laughs*) And
above all, it does not represent either the feminine or the
masculine; it is there to represent that which is beyond. So
establishing something which is of a non-physical nature into a
physical form is a much more complex, much more demanding
process than establishing that which is a force in the process of
creation. The feminine is a force in the process of creation; you

---

28   A manifestation of the Divine Feminine, both fierce and
compassionate at once. The goddess energy is mainly geared towards
bringing physical and material well-being.

can draw it from every piece of creation. This is the reason why almost every Devi Temple (except the Bhairavi Temple adjacent to the Yoga Center, because we have done it in a different way) has an animal sacrifice as a part of it. That is because they are trying to use this life energy from this animal and transform it into a goddess.

Bhairavi is feminine. And like everything feminine, she has no morals. The feminine has no morality. A woman may have it, but the feminine never does. This idea of morals, ethics, codes, all this is purely masculine stuff. When women become like men, they will talk of morality and ethics; otherwise how they feel is all that matters to them. If they feel right, they will do anything. It has always been so; it is not a new discovery. The feminine is like that – if her emotions are fulfilled, she will do anything. All this nonsense of morality and ethics belongs to the world of the masculine. That is why right from ancient times they tried to distribute work accordingly.

In society we need some morality, so we let man handle that nonsense, that PR work. Inside the family, there is no need for morality; we can mingle and merge absolutely. So, no morality in the house, total morality on the street. The masculine walks the street; the feminine in the house. We made this arrangement because we wanted to enjoy freedom from the ethical and moral at least when we go home. Now we have made it the other way around – inside the house too much morality and in the social life no morality. That is because we have stupid logical ideas as to how to conduct life without seeing life the way it is.

Shiva said that if the female population increases and females start participating in those things which are limited and logical, then both the man and the woman die. Neither the masculine will exist in its full force and nor will the feminine. When both of them lose their essential quality, the human race cannot continue, and it will dissipate itself. This is beginning to happen in many ways. But still there is a long way to go. Shiva's sense of time and your lifespan are different. When he says it is approaching, he is talking about a few thousand years. But a few thousand years for a great species, which is capable even of liberation, is nothing. As I keep saying, this (*referring to the self*) is not a small thing. This can behave like a worm if it does not know what it is. But if it begins to know what this is, it is not a small thing. This can even put gods to the yoke.

So the Devi needs constant attention. Every day in the morning you have to make an offering to her; otherwise she will sulk; after that she will become furious. We don't want you to see her furious. A woman may be physically weaker, but when she gets angry she can cause hell to you. Isn't it so? She is not capable of punching you or wrestling you down, but she has a way. (*Laughter*) So Devi has to be attended to every day. But, as I said, Dhyanalinga is not like that. If nobody enters the temple for next thousand years, he will still be the same. He is like Shiva, simply sitting with his eyes closed; if nobody attends to him, no problem. So establishing something like that was definitely far more challenging, far more taxing, far more painful, far more manipulative.

Creating Devi has been a pleasure. We paid small prices. There has been a little bit of impact on my system, but it has been a joy. One thing is because of the nature of who she is. Another thing is – I am choosing appropriate words here because I may have to face the wrath of the one who asked this question, who is a minor Devi by herself, I'm sure. In many ways, it is like if I cut my little finger, I can make a Devi out of it. But even if I take my head off, I cannot make a Dhyanalinga. It was manifested somehow not from this body, but through this. But Devi is not like that; she is delivered by me. So with every piece of my body I can make a Devi. If I remove my little finger, you won't miss it. My ability as a guru will not go away. My ability to throw the Frisbee will not go away. I can even play golf without a little finger. I can eat well. I can do everything. With just a little finger, I can create one more Devi and one more Devi.

So am I belittling her? No. All I am trying to tell you is that she is *Prakriti*; she is part of nature and this (*points to himself*) is nature. I can either pull her out of myself or if I am willing to conduct a sacrifice, I can pull her out of an animal because that is also nature. I thought it was not necessary in the ashram to go in for such sacrifices. Actually, if we create a conducive atmosphere, we can even pull it out of a live animal.

So Devi is a wonderful phenomenon but if I have the necessary support, I can pull out a Devi from every tree, every flower, every human being, and establish her in so many different ways. But we cannot do that with Dhyanalinga. It is beyond my physical prowess to attempt another Dhyanalinga. This body cannot withstand that anymore; it is too old. The Dhyanalinga is not just an important event in my life. The making of the Dhyanalinga is a significant event in the very life of humanity. I would go further and say in the history of existence, because even if humanity dies, even if the planet cracks up, it will still be on.

 "There is enough food on the planet, but half the people cannot eat properly. If the feminine was dominant, the population would eat for sure."

Questioner: How important is Linga Bhairavi, a goddess energy, to our planet today?

Sadhguru: See, the worship of the feminine was prevalent right across the planet at one time. But unfortunately, a certain very ambitious approach to religion, as with everything else, became the mode. When conquest became the mode, people burnt the feminine out of the planet. We made it like this that the masculine is the only way to be successful, and we have compelled even women to be very masculine today in their attitude, approach and emotion. We have made everybody believe that conquest is the only way to success.

But to conquer is not the way; to embrace is the way. Trying to conquer the planet has led to all the disasters. If the feminine was the more dominant factor, or at least if the two were evenly balanced, I don't think you would have any ecological disasters, because the feminine and earth worship always went together. Those cultures which looked upon the earth as the mother, they never caused too much damage to the environment around them. Only when conquest was seen as the way of life did damage happen.

See, right now, after all this damage to the planet, still half the people cannot even eat properly. There is enough food on the planet, but half the people cannot eat properly. If the feminine was dominant, the population would eat for sure. If the feminine was dominant, compassion and love and aesthetics would be dominant.

But we chose the power of gross conquest over the subtleties of love and compassion. We chose to conquer life rather than embrace it. Maybe if the feminine was dominant we would not have gone to the moon or Mars, but what have we really achieved by going there? We just put a flag there, and we came down. We left a footprint there, and we came down. What is the significance? The whole romance of the moon is gone now. (*Laughs*)

So our whole attitude towards life has become very lopsided. I am not against scientific achievements, but we have lost the life-orientation of science. As I said, right now unfortunately science and technology, for most people at least, only means how to use everything on the planet for our benefit. So this attitude of how to exploit everything for our benefit is a very conquest-oriented masculine approach. If the masculine and the feminine were evenly balanced, we would have lived much better lives. Unfortunately we have even compelled women to become masculine in their approach to life.

"That every human being and every creature that walks or crawls should live in a consecrated space is the dream of every enlightened being."

Question: Sadhguru, you mentioned (during the Kailash trek) that at one time the country of Nepal itself was consecrated as a full energy body. How has this been used by the people for spiritual benefits? Are such things possible even today? Can the whole planet be energized?

Sadhguru: This is a tremendous experiment – a successful experiment – that a certain group of beings of phenomenal caliber created. A certain part of Nepal – not the whole country as it is, because it used to be many kingdoms at one time – was made into a spiritual body by itself, establishing shrines at key points. The physical body that you have right now is an accumulation of food. But to convert food into flesh and bone, you need an energy system, an energy body. So, they built a massive energy body across the geography of a certain part of Nepal, so that the whole population could live in a consecrated space.

That every human being and every creature that walks or crawls should live in a consecrated space is the dream of every enlightened being. Similar things have been attempted in Tamil Nadu and in the southern parts of India. They have also been attempted in various parts of North India but, as I mentioned previously, most of it has been destroyed due to invasions. Southern India is, I would say, more intact that way. This is a dream of every enlightened being because it does not matter how many teachings or practices or methods you impart to people, you have to create a womb where people can naturally rejuvenate and grow. For the common populace to be able to do sadhana by themselves, go beyond their physicality and attain to their highest, is not impossible. But unfortunately, most people would not do it because their lives tend to be determined by the natural forces around them.

The whole purpose of spirituality is to transcend all the limitations of nature. It is nature which gave you the body. It is nature which gave you this life, this earth to live on. But now, if you want to transcend her, she is not going to let you pass so easily. So you have to be extremely alert and carry a certain kind of energy so that she cannot hold you. Otherwise she will hold you at every point in a million different ways.

So, creating an energy body, creating a consecrated space in such a way that the very atmosphere around you is constantly instigating you to go beyond your physicality – this has always been the aim. You will see Tamil Nadu is full of this. Magnificent temples were built here. The people who actually built these temples often lived in small hutments. But they built such fabulous temples because they realized that living in a consecrated space is more important than living in a comfortable home. Every street in Tamil Nadu has five temples. These are not in competition with each other, though it may be turning out that way today. The purpose of this is to ensure no creature that walks this land will ever be outside a consecrated space.

This great dream has many times come close to fulfillment and many times it has been pulled down. Once again, we are making such an attempt. If you ask me what my dream is, I'd say I would like to consecrate the whole planet.

CHAPTER 4

GOD'S MINIATURE GODS
The Human Being as Cosmic Library

"...if you closely observe this human system,
everything cosmic is right here in a miniature form."

"The most incredible thing is that you can know everything you wish to know with your eyes closed."

Sadhguru: If you closely observe this human system, everything cosmic is right here in a miniature form. This human system is a cosmic library if you are willing to study it. But people are always busy with something else; they do not pay attention to this one (*referring to the self*). Otherwise, this is like a seed. Everything that is there in the tree, in a minuscule way, is there in the seed. In one sperm and one egg, whatever is needed to make one human being is there in a very minuscule way. If you are willing to look at it, you can draw the picture of the man or woman that will come out of it. If you know how to look at these two cells or these two units of creation closely enough, you can actually make a picture of the person who will come out after twenty-five years.

We know that today we can use genetic mapping and predict what kind of results will happen, subject to various other things. Let's say I plant an apple seed today; tomorrow morning it sprouts and grows up to a certain height. Now a cow may come and eat it up; somebody may uproot it; somebody may drive their car upon it; all those things are possible. But if nothing like that happens, if it gets nurtured properly, right now I can draw the apple tree to show you how it will look after twenty-five years. This body is also just like that. This body exists on a micro level, but if you look at it carefully enough, the macro is written into this. This body can be an incredible possibility.

As I said earlier, with scientific research, as more and more things are being discovered, things are only getting messier, not clearer. If you are interested in knowing life, that is not the way to know it. If you want to use life, that is the way to do it. Using life should not have been the goal of science. But right now science is being funded and it is progressing in a way as if everything in the existence is here to be merely used by us. We have learned to use everything, from the biggest thing, like the planet, to an atom or even a single-celled animal; we even know how to use an amoeba towards our well-being! The larger part of science is aimed at learning how to use everything in the existence for our well-being. The more and more you use everybody's life for your own well-being, you will see well-being is the one thing that will not happen to you. Everything else will happen, but well-being will not happen.

Do you not see that just a few generations ago people were physically better than they are today? Physically, we are at our weakest today, as a generation of people. Our numbers are increasing because all of us survive. There is no natural selection. (*Laughs*) Because of vaccinations and inoculations, hospitals and medical care, all of us survive. All those who would have been nature's rejects, all those people live now. So our population has increased, but physically we are definitely at our weakest. Never before have men and women been as fragile and weak as they are today. Two generations ago people were strong because they had to do an incredible amount of physical activity every day. Today it is not like that; so human beings have become extremely weak.

So we have achieved neither health nor well-being, neither peace nor joy. It is just that we have done a million things with the world; we are doing things that nobody would have imagined. We are even multi-tasking! (*Laughs*) But we cannot do one thing of consequence with ourselves. That is what has happened. It does not matter how much exploration you do with the outside, you will neither know the world, nor will you know yourself. That is the reason why we said that if you turn inward, not only can you know yourself, you can liberate yourself, you can dissolve yourself. You can also know existence the way it is.

This is a very complex and magnificent creation, something way beyond our logical mind's ability to ever perceive. If you want to know the nature of this (*referring to the self*), there is a certain way. Now, the essential reverberation in the human being is in the spine. The subtler the reverberations get, the further it goes. If it gets very subtle, you can just throw it all over the place. Now once your reverberations spread themselves all over the place, your ability to perceive is also all over the place. So right now, what you refer to as "myself," in terms of your limited existence, is whatever is within the boundaries of your sensation. Whatever is within the boundaries of your experience, is "you." Whatever is outside your boundaries of experience, is "somebody else," "something else." By refining your reverberations, you can extend the boundaries of your experience endlessly. So when we say Shiva opened his third eye, this is all it means: he extended the boundaries of his experience in a simply unlimited way. Now the whole existence is just a part of him.

So yoga refers to the human spine as the "*merudanda.*" That means it is the axis of the universe – or at least it can be, if you reverberate in a certain way. So this is an instrument. Are you going to use it just to gather food for yourself? Are you going to use it just to perform feats? Or will you use it in its highest possible capability?

So as I mentioned before, if you want to use it like an instrument, the first and foremost thing is that you dis-identify yourself from your body. You know very well how you gathered this body. There is no question about that. How can you call what you gather as "myself?" What you gather cannot be you, isn't it? It is yours for a certain period of time; that is fine.

For example, the other day the children from the Isha Home School were on a treasure hunt. So this treasure hunt for these little children between ages five and eight was all about food and the human body. They were all very excited about it. And when I drove up they said, "Sadhguru, do you know in one year an individual human being eats 1,100 kilos of food?" I said, "Not me." (*Laughter*) There are people that do, but not me. And another child came up and said, "Sadhguru, do you know in one lifetime we eat fifty tons of food?" Now that is a lot of food. So if you ate fifty tons of food, what should be your weight? If you weigh fifty kilos, what it means is that the remaining 49,950 kilos is shit. Only fifty kilos has remained here. That is a lot of shit. (*Laughter*) So if you consider all your karma as shit, then that is a lot. This body you drop every lifetime and recycle. Karma you accumulate further. That is a lot of shit.

Once it happened. Two crocodiles met. One was looking nice and fat; another was looking like a year-long Samyama[29] program. Now this lake where they lived was next to the court house.

And the skinny one said, "Oh my friend, how do you manage this? Both of us are eating pretty much the same diet, but you look good. Look at me. I am mostly skin and bone."

So the fat one asked, "How do you get your prey?"

The skinny one said, "I go wait at the parking lot where the lawyers park their cars. And when they are just opening their car doors, I go from beneath the car, grab them, pull them under the car, shake all the shit out of them and eat them."

So the other one said, "If you shake all the shit out of them, all that is left is a briefcase."

---

29 Alluding to the advanced eight-day program at the Isha Yoga Center where to call the diet frugal would be an understatement!

That is the mistake. So if we shake all the karma out of you, what is left? Nothing much. (*Laughs*)

So this human body is such a miraculous instrument. If you learn to create a distance between you and the five elements effectively, you have a clear space between you and the body. We want to create the distance between you and the body, just so that you will have the joy of knowing what kind of a machine has been handed over to you. It is not a simple one; it has all the ingredients of bondage and freedom within it. You can make this divine. You can move your energy system in such a way you can turn this body into a deity, or you can be here like a corpse. So you can either make this body into a "*shava*" or a "Shiva." Shava means a corpse. Shiva means the Ultimate. It is just about what you do with it. It can function in ways that you have never believed a human being can function.

If we really want people to realize this, it needs a very unreasonable level of trust and intimacy. You cannot do these things unless you learn to hold your body away from yourself, unless you learn to see this is not "me," unless you learn to see that this body is definitely a magnificent instrument. Then you feel like exploring the full possibility of this instrument.

Suppose you buy yourself a new car and want to see what kind of a machine you have. If you want to test it out, you must give it to a good driver. You could try me. (*Laughs*) If you want to really know the full depth and dimension of this machine, you must give it to somebody who will stretch it to the limits. Then you will see this is not just fifty kilos of shit. This is something else. It has been made in such a miraculous way. If you know how to stretch it to its full length, this body is a ladder to the Divine. Not just a ladder to the Divine; if you know what to do with it, it is the Divine itself.

So I am not known to give water to the thirsty people who come to me. I am known to put salt in your mouths, because if you get really thirsty, you will somehow know. The problem is you are not thirsty enough. You are not willing to invest any time looking inward. And we are so used to making deals with everything in life. We think we can make deals with just about anything. But when it comes to the subjective dimensions of life, your deals will not work. Deals will work with people around you. With this one (*referring to oneself*), you cannot make any deals. Either you open up and know it, or you will not know it. That is all there is.

Once, a hotshot CEO of a major tea marketing company in United States got a bright marketing idea. Those were the days when the Concord was flying between New York and Europe. So he and his secretary got into the Concord and landed in Europe for an appointment with the Pope.

The CEO said, "See Holy Father, just look at me; if you are willing to just say one sentence for my company – in just a ten-second shoot, one take, no retakes – I will donate a quarter of a million dollars for you to do God's work. Are you on?"

So the Pope asked, "What is it, son, that I need to say?"

The CEO said, "You just have to say: Dear God, thank you for our daily tea."

The Pope thought about it – after all, it was a quarter of a million dollars – but he said, "No my son, I don't think I can do that."

The CEO got up, paced up and down and said, "Okay, half a million dollars. Is it a deal?"

The Pope said, "I would like the money for the work that I am doing, but I cannot say that."

"Okay, Pope, one million dollars. Are you on?"

The Pope said, "No, I cannot say it."

"Okay, this is it, man! Five million dollars. Are you going to do it?"

The Pope shook his head. "No."

Then the CEO said, "Okay, it is up to you," and he left.

They hopped onto the next Concord. On the plane, he was biting away at his nails. Then he told his secretary: "I really wonder what the bread people are paying him." (*Laughter*)

There are some things with which you cannot make deals! You just have to keep your deals aside. Don't think, "Okay, I will keep my logic aside; will I experience mysticism? Is that a deal?" No, it is not a deal. First and foremost, if you want to taste the mystical, stop the stupid deals. Can you? You will not get anything, but you are still willing to look at this dimension. Is that okay? Your logic can be kept aside only if you are overwhelmed by a certain experience. At those moments, your logic falls down. Or in a state of very deep trust, you can put your logic down. Without these two things, you cannot put your logic down.

So how do you receive this? Right from the start I have been telling you that when you come and sit here, forget the spiritual nonsense – forget the guru, your nirvana, your mukti, your enlightenment. Just sit here as you would sit in a cinema theater. As it gets more and more exciting, you begin gaping, isn't it? Just sit here like that. A film is simply a play of light and sound, but look at the impact it has on you. You allowed the film to enter you, because you sat aside from yourself. You did not sit there analyzing everything – unless you went as a critic. You just sat there and enjoyed it. That is the best way to perceive things.

So if this has to happen, that is all that is needed. You do not need anything else. You need an open window. You need an open door. You cannot do it, but you can allow it. That is the only way it can happen. We have very little time. And as I said, I am foolhardy. Any opportunity I get I do not want to miss. (*Laughs*)

 "I am not here to speak the Truth. I am here just to give you a method to perceive it."

Questioner: If the whole universe is within, does that mean that it is futile for us to go anywhere or do anything? Does it mean we should stop wandering around, simply sit, look within and see what we can find?

Sadhguru:. At this stage in your life, you should not be wandering around; that is for sure! (*Laughter*)

I did not say the whole universe is within you. I only asked, whether you are a scientist or a spiritual seeker, what is it that you are seeking? You want to know what the nature of this (*referring to the self*) is, isn't it? If you say, "Oh, I am not interested in the whole universe; I am just interested in myself," that is fine. Or if you say, "I am interested in the whole universe," that is also fine. But essentially the nature of human intelligence is such that whatever you do not know, you want to know. Right now you have been kept in a limbo by nature. No matter how intelligent you think you are, you do not know anything about the nature of your existence. Just look at it; you really do not know anything. After so many steps taken by science (which has definitely brought its benefits and comforts), there have been no revelations, isn't it?

So if you go around the universe and come back – which we have tried in so many ways – still you will not know anything. So if you want to know how this universe has happened, you can look inward. How this human system is happening, in the same way the universe has happened. In the same way that the micro is happening, that is how the macro has happened. If you look at the micro and perceive it, you will also know existence. I did not say the existence is within you. In a way that is also true, but I did not say that.

That is because I am not here to speak the Truth. I am here just to give you a method to perceive it. It is not for me to speak the Truth. For one, you cannot speak it anyway. If you do, it is just a story, isn't it? Maybe it is a true story, but still it is just a story.

I had a great grandmother; she lived until she was 113 years of age. People used to say that she is a devil of a woman. (*Laughs*) When you live that long people start thinking like that. She buried her children, her grandchildren, some great grandchildren also. But she would not go. People thought she was a devil of a woman, not because she did anything evil, but because when she laughed, people said she laughed like a devil. When she laughed, the whole street shook. It was a hoot of laughter. If she let it loose, everything reverberated around her. Women of her generation were not supposed to laugh like that. Now, you can laugh like that, but you are not laughing. She did not belong to any generation. She simply laughed. She had seen too much of life. At the age of sixty-four, she left the family. She fulfilled all these so-called "responsibilities" that she was supposed to fulfill, and she buried her husband; she was free. (*Laughs*)

Questioner: She buried her husband?

Sadhguru: Everybody does when they die, don't they? I did not say she killed him. I only said she buried him. (*Laughs*) He worked himself to death, and she buried him. And then she left the family and went and built a small temple for herself in somebody else's land. My grandfather owned hundreds of acres of land. But she went and built her temple in somebody else's land. She was the family's disgrace. She was a thorn in everybody's flesh, because each day if you just think that your mother or grandmother is living on somebody else's land, and then you think, "I am the richest man in town," it is like a pain, you know? A daily pain she was. And you could not ignore or forget her, because people gathered around her. At least if people forgot her, if she had gone away, far away, we could have said she died. But she was right there. (*Laughs*) She did not lift her little finger to harm anybody, but she was considered a devil of a woman because she laughed. And she laughed because she saw life with much more depth than anybody could have imagined, and everybody around her looked like utter idiots to her.

She ran a kingdom of her own. I have not seen my great grandfather; he died long ago. But my grandfather was the richest man in town, and somebody must have told him, "If you feed the poor you will go to heaven." See, the eyes are always on heaven, please understand. (*Laughs*) So every morning he had an attendance book out. All the beggars in the town could come there and be fed. They had to be registered in the book; otherwise they would not be fed. So every day, a little over 200 people were fed in the morning – one full meal for all the beggars in the town.

So in the morning when they came, my grandfather sat at the front of the house and watched, because he wanted to keep accounts of how many people had been fed. It was all being recorded. (*Laughs*) And people came to him, because almost everybody in the town owed him some money. In the morning they would come to settle their interests or loans, or whatever. So many varied things happened in the front of that house. I am sure if he did not have money people would not have come. They came almost crawling in front of him because he had money and power. This was at the front door of the house.

After they were done with the ugly business, they would all generally go to the back door. There my great grandmother would be sitting. She had a certain way of sitting which, if you just looked at her, seemed arrogant. It was simply the way she sat. She never uttered one arrogant word to anybody. But she just struck that kind of posture.

At the front door, your caste and your creed were very, very important. If you were of the right caste, money would be given to you like this (*makes a magnanimous gesture*); if you were of the wrong caste it would be thrown at you. But when they came to the back door, all of them were embraced by this old woman. And most people did not know her name. When she became old, because of a certain sciatica problem, she used to limp a little bit, so people just called her "Kuntamma" – that means "a limping woman." Nobody knew her name because after 113 years, who would remember your name? (*Laughs*)

I have seen her in absolutely exuberant and ecstatic states. She would go into the *puja* room where in Indian households, as the family gets richer and richer, the number of gods goes on increasing. This was a very rich family so we had dozens of gods, all kinds of silver ones, golden ones, gods of every kind. So she would go there. She had very long hair, well below her hips, and she let her hair loose. And she would be singing and dancing, tears flowing down, but laughing like crazy; and she would pick up flowers with her feet and throw them to the gods. Not with her hands – she picked them up with her feet and threw them to the gods. And she would be in absolutely ecstatic states. I did not know why she was doing all of this, but everybody liked to hang around her, because she was exciting – and, above all, she laughed. (*Laughs*)

So she looked very unreasonable – not the kind of person you would want to have in your family because she was trouble. But because she looked inward, she knew things that nobody could ever figure out. She could not articulate this to anybody because there was not one person she could speak to. So she just laughed it out. Everybody looked like an utter idiot to her because what she could see, they could not see.

Now, as I said before, do not try to look inward, do not pursue mysticism, do not look for god, do not seek enlightenment, because you can only seek what you already know. The moment you start thinking "god," "nirvana," "mukti," you are projecting what you know into exaggerated states. As I mentioned before, wherever you go today, people go on saying "God created you in his own image." And because of this one idea human beings are walking like vandals on the planet. Suppose we thought God looked like an ant, we would not have stepped on ants, would we? We would have been extremely careful as to how we walk on the ground, constantly looking to make sure that we do not step on god's miniature versions. If we thought god looks like a worm, we would not have stepped on a worm. But it is because we think God looks like us that we have become so aggressive. We are the only vandals on this planet. That is because we think we are miniature gods. (*Laughs*)

So this idea that "I am created in the image of the God" came about because whichever way creation happened, that whole map of the creation – from its nascent state to its ultimate state – is also written in you. If you look inward, this existence – from its origin to what it is today and what it will be ultimately – is written into this body. The road map is here. So someone looked inward and expressed it in this manner. He said the whole creation is within you; the source of creation is also within you; the very image of creation is you. Some other fool converted it into something more simplistic and said you are made in the image of God. This made people egoistic, and they vandalized the whole world. It is all because of a simplistic understanding of a complex reality.

So what you are doing right now is just trying to simplify this. This is the biggest problem. Constantly people are busy simplifying the Gita, simplifying this teaching, simplifying that scripture; they think they are doing a great service. But once you make it very simplistic it is going to cause more damage than benefit to people.

So I did not say the universe is within you. I only said whichever way the universe has been created, the record of that, the residual impact of that is also recorded in this system. If you look deep enough into yourself, you can see how the creation has happened. On another level, it is true that the universe is within you, because time and space are stretchable and contractible. But that is not what we are talking about right now.

So when we say "exploring mysticism," we are only looking at how to enhance our perception. We are not looking for God; we are not looking for the Truth, mukti or nirvana. We are not looking for anything about which we have an idea. If you have an idea about it and if your idea is right – especially if it is right

– it is no more mystical. When we say "exploring mysticism," we are not talking about what we normally think of as mystical. We are just seeing how to enhance our perception from where it is to the next stage. We are not even talking about the Ultimate. We are just talking about the next stage. Because knowing the boundaries of your limitation is very, very important if you want to stretch it. The moment you sit here and talk about God, you are finished; you are talking about the Ultimate without seeing the next step. It just leads to a hallucinatory way of looking at life.

So let's go slow, okay? One step at a time. Or do you want to go straight to heaven? That is easy; we could shoot you in the head! You would go straight to we do not know where, but you believe that you would go to heaven. (*Laughter*)

 "Even if a boon is given to people, they know how to make a curse out of it, simply because they do not know the very nature of who they are."

Questioner: If the road map of how creation begins and ends is written into this body, how does destiny come into all this? Does destiny exist? Is it also written into this body? Does it play a role in our existence?

Sadhguru: If you are talking about the very destiny of existence, yes. Normally when you raise this question about destiny, you are talking about what will happen to you in this life, right? You are a young person, so naturally you are concerned about your destiny. Old people are concerned about your destiny, because they have no destiny; it is all over. (*Laughter*) You are worried about your future; they are worried about somebody else's future.

So if you are talking about "what will happen to me in this life," whatever you do, whatever you create, will happen to you. Do not wait for it to happen to you. Make it happen. (*Laughs*) When it comes to creating your life, please make it the way you want it. Do not wait for it to happen because of the shape of the stars or where they are going or coming. That is a very poor way to live.

But if you are looking at the destiny of the creation itself, yes, by looking inwards we can clearly say what will happen to this creation. We may not be able to calculate numbers and the exact time, because once you talk about billions of years, whether it is one billion years or one thousand billion years, what is your problem? One billion years or hundred billion years does not make any difference to us. If we are talking one year or ten years, time matters to us, because what matters to us is only always in relation to our own existence. Our lifespan is a question of eighty to a hundred years. So we do not talk billions of years; we just say "eternal." (*Laughs*) One billion years may not be eternal. But as far as we are concerned it is.

Questioner: One question comes to my mind: if everybody looked inward, what would happen?

Sadhguru: You would have a sensible world. (*Laughs*) Is that a danger? Right now we are living in a senseless world. For example, anything that is given to human beings, they are making a misery out of it. They are poor and they are miserable. But you make them rich; they get more miserable. They are uneducated; that is their misery. You educate them; they get more miserable. They are unmarried; they are miserable. You get them married, and...! (*Laughs*) No children; they are miserable. If they have children, they will become miserable. Since life seems to be a misery, we offer you death. But then you will become even more miserable. It does not matter what you do, people are capable of making anything into misery.

Right now, for example, modern technology is a tremendous boon. When technology came into our lives, our lives should have become beautiful, but that has not happened. Our lives have become convenient in many ways, but not beautiful. Our lives are getting uglier and uglier. We are threatening the very life on this planet with our technologies, isn't it? So even if a boon is given to people, they know how to make a curse out of it, simply because they do not know the very nature of who they are. Without knowing the essential nature of this (*referring to the self*), we are trying to make a life outside. That is the biggest mistake humanity has made.

There is a beautiful temple in Karnataka, in southern India, called the Annapurneshwari temple. Behind the temple, in the local language, it is inscribed on the rock how during the pre-Vedic times – which was 6,000 – 7,000 years ago – people knew how to build an airplane, using solidified mercury as a fuel. Today rockets which go beyond the atmospheric limits use solid fuels. It is the latest technology of locomotion. So this inscription talks of using solid fuel in the airplanes; how they can be used for warfare, etc. But in the end the advice given is this: we should not do these things because if we fly these objects, the etheric layer of the earth will get disturbed. If the ether gets disturbed, then human beings will be disturbed (because a certain part of them is ether), and they will go through unnecessary turmoil and lose their mental balance; they will never live well. So we should not fly these airplanes. Now this is wisdom isn't it? We can do all this, but if you do this, these will be the repercussions, so it is not worth doing it. It is great technology all right, but not worth doing it. This should be the wisdom with which we should approach science, isn't it? Otherwise science will not lead to well-being; it will just lead to destruction.

Science is a fantastic tool for human well-being, but unfortunately, it is threatening human life today. Not just human life, it is threatening the very life of the planet because the necessary wisdom and inner strength is not there. Though all these technologies were explored, these people in the past kept it aside and explored only inner technologies. They considered knowing the ultimate within you to be more important than flying an airplane. So they say, let's not fly an airplane, let's sit and meditate. Does it make sense? It will make sense only when tremendous disasters happen, unfortunately. Today, for most people, till then it will not make sense.

The first and foremost thing you must know is this (*referring to the self*). Then you can handle the external like a play, without any effort. Right now people are in a compulsive state. There is a certain desperation to everything they are doing, because if they do not do all these things, they cannot be peaceful or happy. So if all the 7 billion people on this planet keep doing things desperately, there will not be any world left. (*Laughs*) That is all that is happening. So essentially we have to keep fifty percent of the people hungry and starved so that they do not do too many things. If all the 7 billion people used modern technology and became very industrious, I think the planet would last no more than ten to twelve years. So it is our poverty and lethargy which is saving the planet, not human intelligence, love or compassion!

That is not a good way to live, is it?

 "Music...if you know how to enter it, it can become your route towards the very basis of this existence."

Questioner: I have often wondered if there is any connection between music and mysticism. Does music play a special role in meditation, for instance?

Sadhguru: What is sound? Today modern science is proving to you that the whole existence is just a reverberation of energy. Where there is a vibration, there is bound to be a sound. So what we are saying is that, on one level, every form in the existence is just a certain type of sound. Some sounds may be noise; some may be music. If you feed any sound into an oscilloscope (which is a sound-measuring instrument), depending upon its frequency, amplitude and other dimensions of the sound, it naturally gives out a certain form. So every sound has a form attached to it. Similarly every form has a sound attached to it.

So as you can see existence, you can also hear existence, if you wish. When I say hear existence, I am not talking about the sounds that you are hearing right now. I am talking about sounds that you do not hear right now. The whole existence is one big sound. You do not hear all of it. You only hear a certain frequency of sounds – a small band of frequencies. Anything below this small band of frequencies, we call subsonic, and anything above that we call ultrasonic. Both the ultrasonic sounds and the subsonic sounds are not in your audio perception. So what is in your perception is very small. There are other animals, birds and creatures which can hear sounds that you cannot hear. You know elephants communicate in subsonic sounds. They are talking, but you cannot hear them.

So the whole existence is sound. Now, a certain arrangement – a certain beautiful arrangement – of these sounds is what you refer to as music. When sounds are arranged in a certain way that it creates a certain type of impact on you, you call it a certain type of music. Has it got something to do with spirituality? There is nothing in this existence which is not connected to your spiritual process. Everything is. It is from this that Indian culture created this idea (which now might have taken on extreme forms) that if you see a tree, you bow down; if you see a rock, you bow down; if you see a cow, you bow down; if you see a snake you bow down. Whatever it is, it does not matter what. Every creature, every form, whatever you see, if it makes an impression on you, you bow down to it. Some people do it out of experience. Some people do it out of understanding. Some people are just doing it as a ritual. Basically, people saw that, after all, everything is from the same reverberation. So if you bow down to one thing, what is the problem bowing down to something else?

So sound is another form of existence. Based on this is the science of mantra. Mantra means sound. Yantra means a corresponding form. And tantra means the technology of putting them together. So there is mantra, yantra and tantra: sound, form and the technology of using it. It has been used and misused in a million different ways, so it has taken on many variations. But it is a very essential and powerful process.

Music is a kind of mantra because it is a certain arrangement of sounds. Indian classical music has a huge volume of mathematics involved in it. In fact, any music has it. But here there is one kind of very conscious mathematical process. A person who sings classical music is constantly calculating in a very beautiful way. After some time, people may just sing out of their flair for music, but otherwise there is calculation involved in the process. So if you know how to enter this complex arrangement of sounds and the mathematics behind it, music can become your route towards the very basis of this existence.

I think this understanding is there in every culture to some extent. I think the Bible starts with: "In the beginning was the Word, and the Word was with God, and the Word was God." When I sing "Nada Brahma," it means just that. It means the very sound is the Creator, because sound is creation. If you master the sound, you can also master the form.

So sound plays an important role, and you can use sound in many different ways. At Isha, we use sound in a very powerful way. When we take people into different kinds of processes, we use sound in a very big way, because sound is a simple way of breaking limitations and going ahead.

Your question was, "what has it got to do with my meditation?" Don't try to meditate with music. Listen to music, and if music makes you meditative, that is fine. But do not try to mix these two things. Listen to music with total attention; if it makes you meditative, wonderful. But when you meditate, you just meditate.

 "If you are free from memory and imagination, you will always be meditative."

Questioner: At certain times in my meditations, I use my imagination. Is this all right? Or is it not advisable?

Sadhguru: No, do not use imagination in meditation. Imagination is of the mind, isn't it?

Questioner: But I feel a certain energy follows when I use my imagination and it helps my meditation.

Sadhguru: See, everything needs energy. A thought needs energy. If you do not fire it with energy, your thought has no power in it. So imagination also needs to be fired up with energy. That is a different aspect. Right now if you imagine that your third eye is opening up, definitely you will feel some energy, because imagination brings that amount of energy. But you will not really see anything. Whatever you see is just of the mind. You will not see anything beyond the mind, because it is linked to your imagination.

Imagination is firmly rooted in your mind. You must understand this. It does not matter how fanciful or how wild your imagination is, still it is very firmly rooted in your past experience of life. In the Samyama program, because we focus on "Karma Samyama," people have the possibility to touch the unconscious layers of the mind through which past lives are brought into the conscious layers. But if you start imagining, there is no end because you are in a certain state of high energy, and if you just use a little imagination, it gets all blown-up. You will see the mind is capable of creating any number of lifetimes with vivid details, but that is of no significance.

There was a time (before the Dhyanalinga consecration) when we were bringing back people's memories during Samyama, because we were aiming to do certain processes with a few people. But after that was done, I have taken away almost all the memory part of it from the program. What happens is mostly on the level of energy. But it will not come to your memory, because once memory comes, you do not know where memory stops and where imagination begins. It will get mixed up. Actually, if I ask you to tell a story about what you did in your school twenty-five or fifty years ago, you will see that half of it will actually be imagination. You will not remember. Memory and imagination get mixed up somewhere.

Imagination is only to enhance the power of the mind. For people who come from tantric backgrounds, imagination is a powerful tool. When I say "tantra," I know there is a complete misunderstanding of what it is by people who come from outside India. But as I previously mentioned, tantra means a technology. So, the tantric process is a very highly and vividly imaginative process. This is all to acquire a certain mastery and power over certain aspects of life and nature. It is not for somebody who is seeking liberation. Otherwise it is possible that your liberation will also just become imagination! If you are very unfortunate, imagining liberation may carry you right till your deathbed, making you believe things that are not true. If you are fortunate, it will break earlier than that. If real life situations break your imagination, you are fortunate. But if life situations are too well-controlled and you carry your imagination to your deathbed, that is a huge misfortune.

Now, imagination can give you a certain detachment that easily sets you above other people. Suppose you imagine, "Shiva is always with me. Every moment Shiva is with me." Now you will have a new level of confidence. It is like walking through fire – if you walk fast enough, you can walk through fire. (Laughs) Actually most people can walk through fire, but they hesitate. Any sensible man can do it, but most people operate with their fears. If any new situation comes into your life, most of the time the vibes that you send out are those of fear, not of sense. So if you believe Shiva is with you, now you will have a new kind of confidence. But this is not going to liberate you. This gives you confidence; this gives you solace; this gives you a certain sense of integrity which sets you a little above other people. If you want to be over somebody's head, this is okay. But one who is seeking liberation is not aspiring to be on top of anybody else. He is not aspiring to become powerful; that is his power.

There is a very beautiful story in the yogic lore of Karnataka. There was a very wonderful sage; his name was Allamma Mahaprabhu. Allamma inspired a whole genre of saints. These are called Veerashaivas; that means they are like warrior devotees. They are Shiva bhaktas, but they carry arms. They are a very different kind of people, a very wonderful people.

There was another yogi who was on the path of Kayakalpa. "Kaya" means the body; "kalpa" means to get your body into a different dimension altogether. This yogi's name was Siddhalinga. He was also a devotee of Shiva, but he was like a rock.

There are certain kinds of yogas which work towards attaining mastery over the elements. Some people do "bhuta shuddhi" sadhanas. With those kinds of sadhanas, people can make their body like a rock, hard and stable. These are the kind of people who live for 300 – 400 years. They have stabilized their body with their mastery over the five elements in such a way that they continue to live beyond the normal span of human life.

So at the time when Siddhalinga met Allamma Mahaprabhu, it is said that Siddhalinga was about 280 years old. Now Allamma was a very soft and gentle being. He is famous for having written thousands of couplets of enormous depth and dimension. Now Siddhalinga challenged Allamma: "You call yourself a yogi. You call yourself a devotee of Shiva. Show me something you have. What have you got?" Now, because they carry arms, Siddhalinga pulled out a diamond-tipped sword (he was a great warrior), gave it to Allamma and said, "Take this sword and hit me on my head with all your strength. Nothing will happen to me."

Allamma was amused. He took the sword, and with both hands and with all his might he smashed it down on Siddhalinga's head. The sword just bounced off his head. Siddhalinga stood there like a rock. Then Siddhalinga said, "Now that you used this sword against me, I can also use it against you." Allamma also bore arms, so Allamma said, "Okay." Siddhalinga took the sword and slashed it. The sword went right through Allamma. Allamma was like thin air. It just passed through him, and he simply stood there. Siddhalinga swished this way and that way, but the sword went through Allamma again and again. It did not even touch him. Then Siddhalinga bowed down. "I know the yoga of strength," he said. "But I do not know the yoga of gentleness." (Laughs) And he became Allamma's disciple.

So people who want to acquire powers over somebody else, for them imagination is a powerful tool. If you are seeking liberation, if you want to become free, the first thing that you must become free from is your imagination, because that is the deepest trap. Your memory and your imagination are the two traps. Do you see? One of your legs is stuck in memory; another leg is stuck in imagination. If you release yourself from these, meditation is just natural. When you sit for meditation, what is your basic problem? You are either thinking about tomorrow or thinking about what happened yesterday (Laughs), isn't it? If you are free from memory and imagination, you will always be meditative.

So do not fall into either. Memory will bother you. When you sit here, it will come and remind you of your home, your children. When your family is around you, you will be imagining something else – perhaps how to go to a yoga program. (Laughter) When you come to an Isha Yoga program, you will be deeply in love with your family. (Laughs) This is just the trap of memory and imagination.

So do not get into imagination, because if you are using any faculty of the mind, the question of delving into the unconscious nature of the mind does not arise. This must be understood. The mind has no tools to enter the unconscious dimensions. Only if you are outside of the mind you can look at everything the way it is. When you are in it, there is no way to dissect yourself. You can catch hold of somebody else and dissect them, but you cannot dissect yourself. Even if you do, you cannot see everything. If you are using any faculty of the mind you cannot truly be aware of the nature of the mind. People always think imagining God is better than imagining the Devil. It is not true. At least if you imagine the Devil, you will want to come out of it quick. (*Laughter*) If you imagine God, then you do not want to come out of it, isn't it?

All these processes of imagination have been misused by people mainly because they observed certain bhaktas or devotees and they tried to imitate them; that is the whole problem. This must be understood: a very small number of people in the world are truly capable of being devout; all others are conditional devotees.

Poosalar was a poor man, but he wanted to build a magnificent temple for Shiva. So every day he sat, and stone by stone, brick by brick, he went about building this temple in his head. It took him years. Diligently he built it in his mind, really believing he was building it. He finally completed it and planned to open the temple the following day. In the meantime, the king of that country had also built a huge temple for Shiva. He was also opening his temple on the same day. For the king, after some sixteen or seventeen years of construction, the temple was completed. So he was very eager to open the temple for the public on that day. The night before the opening ceremony, he had a dream. In his dream, Shiva came and said, "I am sorry, but tomorrow I cannot come to your temple opening because Poosalar's temple is also opening then. I need to go there."

The king was awestruck. "Where is another temple better than the one I have built? Shiva is going to somebody else's temple!

Who is Poosalar? Find that man." So he went in search of Poosalar. He found Poosalar living in the poorest of the poor localities, in a hut. The king went to him and said, "Where is your temple?" Poosalar said, "What temple? I just have a temple in my heart. I do not have any other temples. I am not a rich man." But the king said, "No, yesterday I had a dream that Shiva wants to come to your temple, not to mine."

Now that is a devotee. He is in a different state altogether. His consciousness is so crystallized that the distinction between what is reality and what is not reality is obliterated. For such a person, if he wants Shiva, Shiva will walk in here. Really, he will physically walk here in front of him. Because his consciousness is so crystallized he has become the Creator. He believes in a certain form, and that form just walks before him. This is not imagination anymore. This is creation.

When Ramakrishna talked about it, it was happening: he was actually feeding Kali and she actually ate the food. That is what it means. He has become the Creator. He is no more a devotee, but he still thinks he is a devotee; that is all. He has obliterated the borders. It has all become one in him. This is a different state of being. Looking at the lives of a few devotees of that caliber, other people are trying to use imagination to become like them. See, when you still have your logical mind intact, do not try to be a devotee. It is a waste of time, because it will not work like that. Once logic is active, it keeps on separating. There is no question of merging.

 "Existing without the necessary awareness to know the nature of your own life is called dreaming."

Questioner: I wanted to know more about dreams and dream states. Are these significant? Is there any mystical or spiritual value in paying attention to your dreams?

Sadhguru: Now, the word "dream" means that which is not true. Or to put it another way, that which is not yet true is a dream. (*Laughs*) Much importance has been given to dreams. And the importance that traditional and spiritual systems gave to dreams has been very badly misunderstood by modern societies. They are trying to interpret dreams in many weird ways which are very life-damaging, life-restricting. Modern psychologists are almost suggesting that a man can live without sleep, but not without dreams! All these conclusions are drawn because they are constantly studying sick people.

So today people are going about saying that you cannot live without a dream; that is the understanding that is prevalent among the psychoanalysts and others. But the whole purpose of yoga is to work towards a state of dreamlessness called "*sushupti*." Sushupti means you are dreamless. You are so aware that you are incapable of dreaming. When we say "dream," we are not just talking about dreaming during sleep, or even what you call "daydreaming." Your very thought process is called a dream. Existing without the necessary awareness to know the nature of your own life is called dreaming. If you do not exist in reality, you are in a dream.

Everything that is happening within the scope of your psychological framework is actually a dream. Dream means that which is not existentially there but which still feels real to you. Anything that is in your experience feels as real, or more real than reality. But since it has no existential basis, it is called a dream. So every thought that you generate is actually a dream. Every emotion that you generate is actually a dream. Or in that context, the whole experience of your life in a certain way is a dream because you do not see anything that is in the world.

Right now if you are looking at me, you do not see me the way I am; you see me as I am reflected in the firmament of your mind. How you see me right now is largely a psychological process, so it is also a dream. I keep telling people, "Just be with me, be with me," because if you simply see me, hear me and believe that you understand what I am speaking, you are still in a dream state, you are still in a psychological process. If it has to become an existential process, you must cut through the psychological. If you can simply be with me and cut through your psychological process and touch another dimension of life, then you are not dreaming. Otherwise you are having a spiritual dream, which is not a good way to dream. (*Laughs*)

Dreams often have more power than reality in most people's lives. That is because they have never really touched reality as such. What they call life is just what they think and they feel, and it is more important to them than the whole cosmic phenomenon. Today, if you have one depressing thought in you, you will sit depressed. Why? The whole cosmos is going on phenomenally well today, but that does not matter. In your mind there is one thought – not too many, just one – that is bothering you, that will depress you and put you in the dumps. This is called a dream. (*Laughs*) Such a great phenomenon, a phenomenon that nobody can fathom, is happening wonderfully well. And if that cannot uplift you and just one single thought of your own making can pull you down, if this is not a dream, what is?

So, the whole purpose of yoga is to move towards dreamlessness. But psychology concludes that you cannot live without a dream.

Now, as a guru, I would just brush all the dreams aside. It does not matter whether you saw God or the Devil, or whatever. If you saw tomorrow in your dream clearly, I would still brush it aside. I would not call it a vision; I would just call it one more dream. It does not matter. Okay, you saw tomorrow; what about it? In what way does it transform you? You only live with more fear, isn't it? So as a guru, I would like to brush all the dreams aside as one pile of rubbish.

But now you are asking academically. If we look at it that way, we can classify dreams into four categories. There are actually five, but we will leave the fifth one alone. About the first set of dreams (I would say almost ninety percent of the dreams in the world are in this category), they are just unfulfilled desires. Modern psychologists are saying you cannot live without a dream because they have always been studying people with so many suppressed desires that they have to find an outlet for their desires through their dreams. A dream is just a way of finding an outlet for all the unfulfilled desires that one has. When one is beyond desire, when one has desires only consciously, never unconsciously, then one is also free from dreaming.

So most of your dreams are just an expression of all the desires which have remained unfulfilled within you. See, the nature of your desiring is such that there is no way you can fulfill all of them in your life, so you have to dream. When you desire compulsively, dream is a safety valve. Otherwise the volume of desires you carry, which are going to remain unfulfilled, will be too defeating. You cannot exist. So you close your eyes. When you fall unconscious, in sleep the mind finds a vent. It dreams of everything you want in exaggerated proportions, and in the morning you feel relieved because all the suppression you created within you with your unconscious desires have been relieved in your sleep. That is more than ninety percent of the dreaming that humanity does.

Almost hundred percent of your dreams do not mean anything. They are just an expression, an outlet for all the unfulfilled desires you have suppressed within you. When I say "unfulfilled desires," I want you to understand, most of the desiring you are not even conscious of. There are so many dimensions of desire in you. On the physical level, on the chemistry level, on the hormonal level, on the mental level, on the memory level, on the imagination level, there are so many kinds of desires within you. Generally, you are only aware of desire on the level of your mind and imagination — also on the level of your body to some extent, but mostly on the level of your mind and imagination. You are not aware of other desires because this whole process of so-called civilization, or culture, or etiquette is just glossing over all these things, just suppressing all these unconscious desiring processes.

If I have to come to very basic aspects of your desiring, you would understand better if I use the analogy of animals. See, for example, a male animal and a female animal are walking. They are not even aware who is male, who is female. But at certain times, some smells emanate from one body and reach the other. Then suddenly they are aware of the opposite sex, and then the longing arises to do whatever they have to do. Now, this is happening with human beings also, all the time. But we have suppressed the very sense of smell, simply because our culture and our civilization would make us feel so ashamed to be living just according to the smells around us. But actually, it is happening all the time. Mentally, you are not aware of it; you are not conscious of it. So, like this, desires are like waves; they keep happening. Not just with smells, but with what you see, with what you hear, because every sense organ can create sensations which will, in turn, create desires.

The second type of dream gives you certain indications of things that could be happening with your body, with your mind and with your immediate life situations – in an oblique way, usually. Now, let's say for example, in your dream you are walking through a forest. I am just giving an example; do not start imagining all these things. You are walking through a forest and you come across a stream, and you find the stream is flowing beautifully. You are watching it, and suddenly it gets blocked by a falling tree. It need not be a logical process, you know. A dream can jump from this to that. Suddenly a dam grows, and this stream gets diverted and is about to flood you. And then something else happens, and the next moment you are flying in the air.

Now, it is very dangerous to say anything about this aspect of the dream, because tomorrow there are many people with active imaginations who will start imagining all kinds of things about their dreams. Basically, the second type of dream is indicating certain things that will happen, but in a very oblique way. Now you saw a stream dammed; then you were about to be flooded away; finally, you flew up into the sky. It could be just that your arteries are blocked and are about to burst the next day. Maybe because of a surgery or treatment, you will again recover. It is possible. You know I am just creating a possible picture. After all, it is a dream; it can be any way. So, it could be indicating something. But it is very dangerous to even suggest this because imaginations will fly.

The third category of dreaming has something to do with the karmic structure. Depending upon the body of karma that you carry with you, accordingly it reflects upon the mind. Very few people relax into very deep states of sleep. Very few people are capable of sleeping truly deeply; they just sleep on the surface. Generally, only children do; children below twelve years of age are capable of sleeping much deeper than the adults. But if you go into that childlike kind of sleep, the karmic structure, or the content of the karmic material may find reflection in your mind. Then you may be seeing things which are from the past. It is possible.

But now you being afraid of swimming in a cave, for instance, has nothing to do with anybody's karma. Most people are afraid of a dark place and water. It is one thing to swim in an open pool; it is a totally different thing to swim in a dark, enclosed pool. Drowning always involves suffocation. Closed spaces, even if there is enough air to breathe, also bring an almost physical experience of suffocation. Have you noticed this? Even if there is enough oxygen to breathe, if it is a hundred percent dark, people's breath will go into a fit. Have you noticed this happening?

I used to take our ashram residents for treks, and one particular trek we would do is a very beautiful one in the Western Ghats in India. It is a thirty-six kilometer trek. On this trek, we would walk on a railway track, which has been lying abandoned for the last six or seven years now. In these thirty-six kilometers, there are over 300 bridges and over a 100 tunnels; some of the tunnels stretch well over one or two kilometers. So I used to

take the people through the railway track. When we went into
the tunnels, nobody could use the flashlight. You could not see
the other end. It was so dark that you could not see your hand.
You do not know whether your eyes are open or closed, that is
how it was. And you would have bats whooshing all over you.
You know, they never crash into you because they hear; they do
not see. Being a railway track, the ground was uneven. Just
walking through this was a very wonderful experience for
people. They would come out thoroughly cleaned up. (*Laughs*)
Some of them would walk through it joyfully singing, so I
would tell them, "No singing, no talking," because by
producing these sounds you are trying to avoid the darkness.
You want to feel the company around you. I would tell them,
"Walk quietly as if you are alone, just feeling your way with a
stick. You do not know where the next step is. You do not
know whether it is the end of the world, or there is another
piece of earth in front of you. Just walk." Walking these two
kilometers, lots of people took almost an hour.

Now if you just walk like this, not knowing where the next step
is, spiritually, it is a very powerful experience. The whole
spiritual process is just this: that you are willing to take the
next step not knowing where it will lead you. If you are not
ready for that, that means you are not ready for any new
possibility. You must just dream. Dreams are not about the
new; dreams are just about recycling the old with new paint.
Your dreams are coming from the body of memory that you
carry within you. Nothing new happens.

So the third dream could be a reflection of the karmic body. But
for a simple fear that you might have about death and
suffocation, don't try to connect it to something from a
previous life. Do not worry about past lives. Do not believe in
them in the first place, because they are still not in your
experience. I am repeatedly telling you this because this is one
simple fact people have not grasped properly. Do not assume
anything that you do not know. It is such a simple thing, but
people have to assume so many things to make themselves
complete. You have to imagine past lives and future lives to

make yourself substantial. Maybe there is no past life; maybe there is no future life. Maybe life is just this, isn't it? Just because somebody talks this nonsense, don't believe it. Don't disbelieve it either. Just keep looking.

The fourth type of dreaming is not really a dream, but it falls into the category of dreams. It is not in the normal perception of most of humanity. We could call it "crystallization." It means crystallizing something that you hold in your mind, or projecting your mind so powerfully that it becomes a reality, a living reality, where something or somebody actually becomes physically present. This cannot be called a dream, but since it has no existential basis, it is still a dream. So as I said before, usually people on the path of devotion experience this.

Devotion means going absolutely crazy with your emotions. When you become a devotee, the emotional part of the mind is fired up beyond its normal limits. That is why devotion has been such a powerful way to the divine. If you just go a little crazy and come down, that is not devotion. But just going all out, totally crazy is something else. Socially, you will be branded as crazy. All devotees were branded as crazy in their own lifetimes. It is only after they are gone that they are worshipped as saints and sages. But in their lifetimes, usually they were branded as crazy.

Most people definitely thought Ramakrishna was crazy. Ramakrishna actually fed food to Kali, and she ate! He fed from the plate, and the food actually disappeared. For Ramakrishna, Kali came, ate with him, talked to him; she was there. You have heard of Mirabai[30] who worshipped Krishna. For Mira, Krishna came and lived with her. He slept with her. They made love to each other. It was not her imagination. It was a reality for her. So this is another kind of dream.

As for the fifth – I have no logical means to express that. Let us leave that alone. Let's stay with these four kinds of dreams.

---

30   A 16th century princess from Rajasthan. A passionate devotee of
      Krishna whom she regarded as her husband.

One is suppressed desires finding expression, which is the main kind of dream that people have. Another is a dream that sometimes subconsciously gives you a glimpse of what could be coming next (which is generally passed off as a vision or an oracle). The third is when you are in a certain state of relaxation, your mind could reflect the karmic body, or the content of the karmic body. The first kind of dream will anyway happen, because there are so many unfulfilled desires. It does not mean anything. The second and third, you ignore. Do not try to make anything out of a dream, because it is too much in bits and pieces. There is no completion to it. The dream itself is in bits and pieces and what you remember is a smaller bit of it. Trying to make meaning out of it will lead you to confusion and distraction.

So do not try to make anything out of your dreams. Just enjoy them. If you have good dreams, pleasant dreams, that is fine. If you have nightmares, horror movies are going free for you. Enjoy them anyway. What is the problem? If you can manifest the fourth kind of dream, it will lead to liberation. Then the mind can become a tool to take you very close to freedom. The mind can take you to a place which is just one step below salvation if your projections become so powerful that they are like reality. It is more real than real. But for that you need devotion.

Modern education is making devotion almost impossible. The modern ways of thinking and the way the whole society is being cultivated, everything is all about you, isn't it? Life is all about you. When you have cultivated your mind like this, it is better you do not dabble with devotion, because you may just waste your time again. But if you are capable of devotion, then you would see emotion – the juicy part of your mind – could turn into an enormous tool in transporting you from the limited to the borders of the unlimited. It does not take you beyond. The mind can never take you beyond, but you could use the mind as a process, as a vehicle to take you to the very edge. Then you have just one more step to take.

That is why devotion is always the quickest way to grow. From here to there is just one single leap. You are there at that border. But the path of devotion is only possible for very simple, innocent minds. Doubting minds, thinking minds, suspicious minds should not pretend devotion. It does not work. You must wait to get the complex portions of your mind beaten down by life. (*Laughs*) Life will beat your mind slowly, very slowly. You will see. You had many ideals; slowly life beats them down, isn't it? One by one, they are beaten down. If you are intelligent, you can sit here, and you can beat all of it down right now. Now when devotion has come as an inner experience, it just bursts forth out of you. You cannot help it. When devotion happens like this, then it transports you from this end to that end very quick. It is the quickest vehicle to transport you.

So whatever kinds of dreams you have, just learn to enjoy them. Do not try to create meaning out of them. They are good visuals. What does it matter what they say?

Questioner: What about "lucid dreams?" What do they mean?

Sadhguru: You are a good dreamer – that is what they mean. Lucid dreaming means you have a continuous cinema. It is okay. What does it matter whether it is lucid or disjointed? That is why I said, "Don't try to categorize them." The moment you categorize them, you will place one above the other. You cannot help it. Once you place one above the other, you will aspire for the superior one. Once you aspire for it, your imagination will run wild. Leave the dreams to happen by themselves, whatever kind of dreams you have. If you have nightmares, do not try to change them. Learn to enjoy the horror movies. Usually late night most of the channels are running horror movies. So you are on one of the channels. So what? (*Laughs*)

"The less you try to influence your children, the more they get influenced by you."

Questioner: Sadhguru, I have a question about birth. You have said before that a person's karma makes her/him settle down in a womb with similar kinds of tendencies and attributes. Then how come two children born to the same mother can be so different? Mothers often experience great joy bringing up one child and great agony bringing up another.

Sadhguru: This opens up too many things. Now when we utter the word "karma," we are not talking about you being punished for your activity or you being rewarded for your activity. That is a silly idea. The word "karma" literally means action. We are referring to past action. What are the types of activity you can perform? You can perform physical activity, mental activity, emotional activity and energy activity. You are active on all these four levels. Every single action that you perform – either with your body, mind, emotion or your energy – leaves a residue, a record of itself.

So without these accumulated impressions, this accumulated heap of information, you would not have any particular characteristic to yourself. You would be "a-characteristic"; you would be without any sense or idea as to what kind of person you are. There would not be any personality. Only because there is a bank of information, there is a personality. So this is just accumulated information. Or this is just an unconscious software that you have created.

Now if karma means action, whose action does it refer to? Yours. It simply means: "This is my action. There are many aspects of life I am unable to understand, but whatever happens to me has to be my karma." That means it is your unconscious action which is producing whatever result right now. Physical existence always happens as cause and effect. Right now you are either enjoying the effect or suffering the effect, but can there be an effect without a cause? It is just that you might have become so shortsighted that you are unable to see the cause. But without a cause there cannot be an effect. This cause is referred to as karma.

Karma goes far beyond your present levels of understanding. Let's not go into that. But from the moment you were born to this moment, all the activity that you have performed physically, mentally, emotionally and energy-wise, isn't it ruling your life right now? The very way you think, feel, understand and experience your life is dependent on your karma. Right now the very way you understand the words that I am speaking depends on your karma. According to your karma, you have a certain interpretation of what I am saying. So karma is deciding everything about you. This karmic process is alive and on; it is stored on many different levels. It is stored in your memory; it is stored in your body; it is stored in your sensations; it is stored in your life energies itself. The very life energy carries the information.

You know our information technology, from the stone tablet days to the present day of blue chips, has come a long way. There was a time when we had to carve everything on stone. Today what could go into a billion stone slabs is going into one little chip. This may sound a little farfetched right now, but the day will not be far off when we find a way to store information in the energy itself. I am saying this because this is how my body is. This is how life is happening within me. The very life energy carries information. If I initiate you into a certain process, you will see each person's energy responds in a different way to the same initiation, depending upon how it is already programmed. Different people go in different ways. Have you seen people who have been in the Isha programs? Each person goes his own way depending upon how his energies are programmed.

So what you call "karma" is unconscious software that you built on all levels, from body to mind to sensation to energy. If you lose your body, you do not lose your karma. If you lose your mind, you do not lose your karma. For most people, whatever happens, they do not lose their karma because there are too many backup systems. So when a person dies, he may lose his body; he may lose his conscious mind. But still the karmic body keeps going in its own way. It is just that the discretionary power will be gone. Because the discretionary power goes, the being functions according to tendencies. Whatever the accumulated tendency is, according to the information that is gathered or the karma that is within, accordingly it finds its way. If you have pleasant information within you, your pleasantness will be enhanced because there is no discretionary mind to spoil it.

Suppose yesterday you passed an examination or yesterday you got married. This information is there with you; it is your memory. If I wipe off the memory, you will not know whether you are married or not. Let's say yesterday you got married; this information is fresh in your mind. Now because the whole society has told you, "if you get married you will be happy," you become happy. Later on they reveal the other things to you, but at least in the beginning they tell you when you are married, it is bliss. This information is there, and that is why you keep yourself very happy. Just take away this information, and you will not know whether marriage brings happiness or not.

So this information is influencing you and keeping you happy right now. But if the person that you married does something that you do not like, then especially because of the information ("I am married, and I am supposed to be happy"), that little thing that the person did gets magnified in a huge way. If you were not told that marriage is bliss, if they had told you right from day one that marriage is about misery, then if somebody did some nasty thing, you would think, "Anyway, this is what it is supposed to be like; it is okay. At least he is not too nasty." (*Laughter*) You know in some societies people are prepared for this. They are told, "When you get married so many horrible things will happen to you. Do not get disturbed; everything will be okay." Such people do not get very disturbed. But there are other people who have been told about marital bliss; their expectations are big. If that bliss does not happen, they crash and the misery is magnified.

As long as the discretionary mind is there, whatever happens, you can still use your discretion to go beyond that. But once the body is dropped, once the discretionary mind is not there, the tendencies rule. Traditionally, we refer to these tendencies as "*vasanas.*" "Vasana" literally means fragrance or smell. So whatever kind of garbage you have within you – I am sorry, whatever kind of flowers you have within you (*Laughter*) – whatever kind of smell, that is the kind of life you attract to yourself. That is the kind of space which you naturally move towards.

So if you are functioning unconsciously, your karma rules absolutely. If you bring a certain level of awareness into your life, the power of karma over your life weakens. But when you are talking about life beyond the body, there is no discretion. So at this stage karma rules absolutely. If you have pleasant karma inside of you, it gets magnified and you become very pleasurable. This is what we refer to as heaven. Heaven is not a geographical place. It is right here, but the problem is you are in hell. In this world also some people are in heaven, and some people are in hell. Isn't it so? We sit in the same place; one person is experiencing heaven, and another person is experiencing hell right there next to him. So it is not a geographical place; it is an inner state. Similarly, if there is pain and misery, then that also gets magnified because there is no discretionary mind to avoid that. Right now if something happened that you do not like, you do become miserable, but then you can employ your discretionary mind and say, "This is enough, let me get out of this nonsense." Then you can come out of it. But suppose you have no discretion, now this misery gets magnified a million times over; that is hell.

So when you start seeking a womb, you tend to move towards a particular type of womb, according to your tendencies. It is a selection. You are actually choosing your womb, but unconsciously. You can also choose it consciously. In India, this is very common (everywhere in the world it is there to some extent): when a person is dying, he should read the Gita or say "Ram, Ram." It does not matter what kind of life he has lived until then. The idea is to create some kind of pleasantness, because at least in that last moment of transition from life to death, if you create pleasantness, pleasantness can become the dominant quality in you. That is the idea.

At the same time, the other possibility is also there. This has happened in the past: certain kings, when they wanted to put their enemies to death, put them through all kinds of experiences. The idea was to create desire. They would get naked women in front of them. They would sexually arouse them, and then kill them. The idea was that the enemy must die in a state of desire so that he suffers a long hell. We know all the technologies, I want you to understand. (*Laughs*) People actually did this. Everywhere they have some understanding of this, and they do it in their own ways. In the Indian culture all these things were explored in detail.

So when this life begins to choose a womb, it is going by tendency. That is unless a being has come to such a level of consciousness that he can choose consciously, which is rare. If he were that conscious, he would have dissolved. It is very rare that he has reached such a point of consciousness and is still choosing a womb. Except those beings, the rest will choose by tendency.

Questioner: So why is the same womb penetrated by two different types of karmic substances?

Sadhguru: There are many aspects to this. One aspect is that very elaborate care was taken about these things in India. In the Indian culture, whatever day the couple got married, that day the woman conceived. Maybe not anymore. Today the pill has come; different contraceptives have come. Otherwise the date for her wedding was always chosen in such a way that it was the best time of the month for her to conceive. It was always fixed like that. So a whole atmosphere was created that was as pleasant as possible, as loving as possible, as beautiful as possible, so that the conception itself happens in a certain pleasantness. People may still be doing this to some extent, but they are not conscious about it. They are doing it as simple rituals.

So that is one factor. If conception has happened in a certain state of pleasantness – either of joy or love or simply pleasantness – it will attract a certain type of life. If it has happened in a certain state of unpleasantness, it can attract a different type of life. But this does not mean that one child is going to be good and the other child is going to be bad. That is not the way it is. See, right now if you have a mango here, a fly will come to it. If you have a lump of shit here, for that also the fly will go. So the fly goes for both. You cannot determine that it will come only for sweetness. No, just because it is the opposite, it may come. Into the womb of a very disturbed and demented person something most beautiful may come, because it may be seeking the opposite. So you cannot decide on that basis alone. But some tendency is driving that life to that womb. It is not for you to go about judging.

So you wonder, "Because I have this kind of child, am I this kind of person?" In spite of you, the child may be wonderful. (*Laughter*) It may not be because of you. You are the way you are because of you. The child is the way he is because of himself. But because he comes to you in such a tender state, you have the capability to influence him to some extent. You can either enhance his pleasantness or enhance his unpleasantness. This option you have, but not totally, never totally. Nobody can make their children a hundred percent the way they want them to be. The less you try to influence your children, the more they get influenced by you. The more you try to influence them, the less they are influenced by you, always.

"This idea – that a human being can evolve beyond his present limitations – and the needed technology to fulfill this idea, is the greatest contribution that Adiyogi, Shiva, made to human consciousness."

Questioner: How do we know if by whatever action we perform we unwind or create new karma?

Sadhguru: So, if the action sinks deeper than the four dimensions, physical, mental, emotional and energy, then we call it kriya. Kriya also means action. As I already mentioned, karma is that kind of action which will leave residual impact upon the system; that means the memory of that action remains, the chemistry of that action remains. Kriya is a type of action which imprints itself on a completely different dimension and begins to dismantle the karmic impact or the karmic residue that has been accumulated in the system, but it is also action.

That itself, in a way, clears up your question. But karma, as I already mentioned, is of many kinds, many layers and many different dimensions. Karma means the imprint of action which remains within you, and karma goes back far beyond your present level of understanding. The actions that your father performed are working and kicking up within you in so many different ways – not just in your life situation but in every cell in your body. Not so easy to get rid of your parents! (*Laughs*) They act up from within. Your grandfather is still kicking within you; your great-grandfather is still kicking within you in so many different ways.

Many of you may be noticing this: when you were eighteen, twenty years old, you completely rebelled against your father or your mother, but by the time you are forty, forty-five, you are beginning to behave just like them – you speak like them, you act like them, you are even beginning to look like them. Have you noticed this? That is a hopeless way to live because if life is going to repeat itself, if this generation is going to behave, act, live, and experience life just the way the previous generation did, then this is a wasted generation. This life, this generation, should experience life in a way that the previous generation never even imagined. The way you experience life can be completely altered; it can be taken to the next level of experience. That is how it should be – unless your father happens to be an enlightened being or in a very evolved state of consciousness. But even if that is so, it is still possible to stretch yourself beyond the point where the last generation stopped.

Now, karma means it is not just yours, not just your father's, not just your grandfather's. The first life form, that single-celled little piece of life, that bacteria or virus or whatever you call it, that one's karma is also acting up within you, even today. Do you know that in a normal-sized body you have approximately ten trillion human cells, but over hundred trillion bacteria? You are outnumbered ten to one. Do you know this? In terms of body weight, if you are hundred kilos of weight, fifty-two kilos of that is probably bacteria. You are more bacteria than human cells. Just upon your facial skin, just upon your face there are eighteen billion bacteria right now crawling on your face. Aren't you glad you are not seeing it? (*Laughter*)

And even the kind of bacteria that you have carries a certain behavioral pattern, depending upon what kind of bacteria your father and your grandfather had. If we are not connected by blood, the way the bacteria behaves in this body and the way the bacteria behaves in some other body out there is very different, depending upon this memory. So you are even inheriting bacteria with a certain quality! Even they are carrying a certain karmic content, and behaving in a certain way, and making the quality of your life in a certain way. You have to transform a hundred trillion bacteria within you to really feel transformed. How is that? So all the grand ideas that you have about yourself are false. This is why we told you, it is all maya, you know (*Laughs*), because the way things are playing within you is such that almost everything that you do is controlled by past information.

Today we know this scientifically, but mystics have always known this: the fact that the memory of that whole life process from a single-celled animal to the human form (which is the highest level of complexity upon this planet) is still there in this body. Or to put it another way, the texture of life in that single-celled animal is still present in this body. Nobody can shake that off.

So, you wonder, "Does it mean to say I am hopelessly entangled?" Entangled for sure, but not hopelessly. In the yogic system there is a beautiful story about Shiva. There is a temple in Kathmandu, called the Pashupatinath temple. Shiva was a Pashupata. Pashupata means a composite expression of animal nature. If you take all the animal forms and see them as a heap of development (from the lower level of animal nature to higher and more complex forms), a human being is on top of this heap. Being atop this whole heap of animal nature means you're a composite expression of all this. If you look at a worm, it is just a worm; if you look at an insect, it is just an insect, a bird is just a bird, a dog is just a dog, an elephant is just an elephant, an animal just an animal. But what you call a human being is capable of all these things. On a certain day you are capable of biting like an ant. Another day you are able to growl like a dog. Another day you can bulldoze through people like an elephant. Another day you can tweet like a bird. You are capable of all these things. At different levels of awareness, human beings become different things. So Shiva was a Pashupata, a composite expression of animal nature, and he became a Pashupati, which means he strived and went beyond his animal nature. So the fact that he rose beyond animal nature is celebrated in the form of a temple.

This is the most significant contribution to human consciousness: just the idea that a human being need not live within the framework that he naturally comes with when he is born. If he strives, he can go beyond this framework and touch a completely new dimension of life. This idea – that a human being can evolve beyond his present limitations – and the needed technology to fulfill this idea, is the greatest contribution that Adiyogi, Shiva, made to human consciousness.

So this huge volume of memory exists within your system, not all of it in the form of living memory but in so many different ways. You can at least see this much: that somewhere inside your body, your body remembers your parents, or sometimes your grandparents, or maybe even your great-grandparents whom you have not even seen and do not know. If you look back, you will see suddenly you have your great-grandfather's nose, your great-grandmother's complexion. At least when the ailments come, you know! The other qualities you may ignore because you're enjoying them, but when suffering comes you naturally look back and ask, "Who gave it to me?" You don't understand that everything that you are enjoying – your intelligence, your capability, your body structure, everything – came from them. You never bow down to them for giving you all this. Only if they give you diabetes or Alzheimer's, you look back and ask, "Who gave this to me?"

Your body's memory goes way beyond your present levels of understanding. It transcends human form, and even animal nature; it goes right back to the basic elements. It is because of this that in yoga the most basic form of sadhana is bhuta shuddhi. As I mentioned before, bhuta shuddhi means to cleanse the five elements. You cleanse these five elements of all memory of your father, of your mother, of your grandparents, of your forefathers, and of that single-celled animal. You erase this memory so that you are your own possibility.

It is from this understanding that when somebody takes to the spiritual path with any seriousness, when somebody gets initiated into brahmacharya or sanyas, they do death karmas[31] for their living parents. This is not a wish that their parents must die. This is a declaration that, "I am going to become free even from my genetic influence. I am taking my destiny into my

31 Death rites that children conduct for their deceased parents.

own hands. My genetics, my chimpanzee past, is not going to rule me. I am moving towards liberation. It doesn't matter how entangled my father was, how entangled my grandfather was, how entangled the chimpanzee was, how entangled every other form was – whose memory I am in the form of this body. Knowing that I have all this memory, I am now declaring I want to become free from it. I am taking the needed steps to walk away from this memory. I am walking away from this bondage to craft my own journey towards my liberation. I am not being ruled by the past." This is the declaration a sanyasi or a brahmachari is making when he takes those steps.

So memory is playing an unbelievable role in just about everything. The way your heart beats is because something within this system remembers how to beat. The way the complexities of chemical reaction are happening within this system is simply because something remembers, "This is the way to do it." This is not something that dropped upon you; this is a learnt process over millions of years of evolution. Life still remembers. If it forgets, you will fall dead right now. So the spiritual process is about distancing yourself from this memory – not destroying it – so that this memory becomes an asset but not a bondage; this memory becomes a dimension which propels you ahead not a dimension which shackles you down. So, from being a Pashupata, a composite expression of animal nature (starting from that single-celled animal to the highest one), there is a possibility of being a Pashupati, rising beyond the animal nature. One can leave all this behind and transcend.

Now, as I already mentioned, if you look at the basic energy skeleton of the human system, the basic blueprint of energy has 112 chakras or junction points where it is held together. This is what you are trying to strengthen when you do Shakti Chalana Kriya[32]. You are trying to strengthen every junction point so that this becomes a solid framework. So tomorrow if you want

---

32 A powerful Isha Yoga practice that moves one's energies. A set of kriyas that is supportive for one's health and creates a strong energy foundation, paving the way for higher levels of perception.

to do something bigger you have the necessary foundation to hold.

Right now the way most people are made, if you initiate them into a strong kriya yoga process, they will break, because they have not prepared the foundation substantially. In many ways, as I have said before, this generation of people is the weakest generation in the history of humanity, both physically and energy-wise. Physically for sure; you cannot dispute it, isn't it? If you want to know what strength is, join somebody who is working on the field tomorrow, and you will see that in two hours' time you will be completely exhausted and the next morning you won't be able to get up. That's how your body will feel. But day after day, he is able do it because that strength is built over a period of time.

So the kriyas strengthen these 112 chakras, which are within the physical framework of the body. But all these chakras function according to the influence of the karmic residue, which is there within the system. The system is not completely free. If you keep it vibrant, it will allow you to transcend many times, but it is not completely free. The karmic residue or the past memory which makes this life process happen controls these 112 chakras. They function within the framework of the karmic influence.

But there are two other chakras, the 113th and 114th, which are outside the physical framework of the body. They generally remain very minimal or almost dormant in most people, but if you have done enough sadhana, they become active. The 114th chakra pulsates in a certain way which, right from ancient times, has been described as the "Ouroboros." Ouroboros is the symbol of a snake eating its own tail; that is, it is trying to swallow itself. Have you seen this symbol? In India, all over the temples you can see it. But you can also see this in Greece, in Egypt, in Mesopotamian temples, almost everywhere. In all those ancient cultures which were focused more upon the beyond than what is here, you will see the symbol of Ouroboros, where a snake is trying to eat its own tail.

So the 114th chakra pulsates in the form of an Ouroboros. And today, I don't know how they arrived at this, but mathematics uses this sign as a sign of infinity. So the 114th chakra pulsates in the form of the infinite, and if your energies touch this dimension, then every action is a process of liberation. If it's within the 112, every action that you do has a residue, so it is best that you do the right kind of action so that it leaves a pleasant residue upon you. But someone whose energy transcends the 112 and resides mostly in those two chakras which are beyond the physical framework, he need not bother about his actions. He can act whichever way he wants. Whichever way he acts, it only leads to his liberation because the action is not his anymore; it is of infinite nature.

So whether activity is entangling or activity is a process of liberation essentially depends on one's level of sadhana and also the attitude and the volition with which the action is done. If people try to do sadhana without performing the needed activity in their lives, sadhana will be a great struggle. Suppose you come here and I tell you, "You don't need to do anything. Just sit, we will take care of you. Twelve hours a day, just sit and meditate." Initially it may look like a great fortune, but after a month's time you will be going nuts. If you cross that madness, you will cross everything. But most people give up when the madness arises within them. You will freak and try to run away because it's not going to be easy. You'll hear the primal cry of your father, your grandfather, your forefathers – and the goddamn bacteria! All of them will scream to find expression. They won't keep quiet. Millions of lives will scream from within; they want to have their say; they want to live through you. They won't let you go free just like that. Parents are demanding, isn't it? If you say, "I want to do something," they'll say, "No, you are my son, you have to do what I want you to do because I have to live through you. All my dreams have to be fulfilled through you." This is not just something they are saying verbally; from within they will scream.

One way to deal with them is to obliterate them (which is a hard path, which needs a lot more sadhana), and another way is to distance yourself. Let them scream; you put on earplugs and you are not bothered because you don't hear! These are two different ways. But you cannot ignore them. You cannot ignore them because they throb in every cell in your body.

So as I've said already, karma is not just things that you did, good or bad. Karma is the memory of life. The very way the body is structured depends on that memory of life. Do you know within your brain there is a reptilian brain which is almost the size of a brain of a crocodile? Do you understand why you go snapping at everybody? (*Laughter*) Because the reptilian brain functions from within you; you can't help it. It is a medical fact that you have a reptilian brain. So the venom (*Laughs*) is not accidental; it is there.

To distance yourself from all that takes a little bit of work, or simply devotion. If you have to do it by yourself, it needs a lot of work. If you want to ride the grace, no work, but you are not in the driver's seat. Either you learn to drive, which involves many risks. Or an expert driver will drive, and you sit and doze off in the back seat. Some people went to Kailash, and through the most treacherous terrain, they were like this. (*Gestures nodding head*) (*Laughter*) They saw Kailash. I drove all the way, alert every moment (otherwise you'll get killed) and I saw Kailash. So what's the big difference? As long as you get there, what does it matter how?

Questioner: Talking about karmic memory and dream, you had spoken during the three-month Anaadhi Program[33] in the US about fast-forwarding dreams and evolving a dream yantra to enable this to happen. What are the benefits of such a yantra?

---

33   A ninety-day residential program conducted by Sadhguru in 2010 at the Isha Institute of Inner-Sciences, USA, in which over 200 participants underwent powerful spiritual initiations.

Sadhguru: The dream machine, or the dream yantra, is a tool to hasten that part of the dream which in yoga we call the "*linga sharira*." Probably in the English language we can call it the genetic body. So, as I said, this genetic body or the linga sharira has a memory of its own and this memory continuously plays.

The effort during Anaadhi was to compress the linga sharira to a very small size. When it is compressed, it becomes concentrated. When it becomes concentrated, the spiritual process could be very overwhelming for people, because this vast memory, which was spread out, is now concentrated. Many people may not be able to handle that kind of situation; they need to be in a very protected atmosphere. If they are not in a protected atmosphere it just cannot happen. But even in a protected atmosphere it can be very overwhelming.

So the idea was to reduce the content of the linga sharira, to reduce the volume of the memory, so that the shrinking did not become too overwhelming. We set up a dream machine or a dream yantra to hasten the process of the dreaming. So the participants slept well in the night and still got up very exhausted in the morning! That's because the dreams were moving at such a rapid pace that their rest time was the most exhausting. People got up totally exhausted because they had been dreaming so hard. But this was done to reduce the volume of the linga sharira; otherwise the compression of the linga sharira would become very difficult and overwhelming.

All this was in preparation of a sadhana called "*linga sanchalana*," that is to activate the core linga within. As a build-up to this linga sanchalana kriya, we wanted to compress the linga. To compress the linga we had to reduce the volume of memory. That's why we set up this dream machine.

You may ask, "What is the use?" The use is that we are not touching your *prarabdha karma* or the allotted karma for this lifetime. We are only going for the entire warehouse of karma, or the *sanchita karma*. So the dream yantra is only for those people who have decided that they want this to be their last time around. If you have a desire for a little more food, for a little more pleasure, if you want to watch one more film that is produced in 22nd century (because they're going to do 4D, you know?), then you should not go in for it. Because once the sanchita karma is taken off, this life will become incapable of taking on one more body, even if it wishes to. But the prarabdha is untouched.

So you don't see any immediate transformation in the person, because, as I have said before, changing attitudes – becoming a little gentle, a little loving, a little compassionate – is not a spiritual process; it is a psychological and social process. The spiritual process means you dismantle the physical nature. You dismantle it in such a way that it doesn't lead you to ill-health or death, but still it is dismantled. That is what a dream machine is about: the substance that is necessary to form one more body, to find one more womb, has been taken away, but this body is perfectly fine. If you touch the prarabdha karma then this very body will start working itself towards dissolution. So we don't touch the prarabdha karma; we just take away the sanchita.

That means we've destroyed your future. (*Laughter*) You get me? But your present is intact.

 "*When someone leaves his body consciously, he is truly no more. That is referred to as mukti or liberation. The game is up.*"

Questioner: So after all this memory is shed, what happens? What is ultimate liberation or mahasamadhi? We have heard stories of yogis shedding their bodies in mahasamadhi. What exactly does it mean?

Sadhguru: Many yogis choose to leave their bodies. They will say, "On this day, at this time, I will leave my body." They will sit down in front of everybody and just walk out of the body. Without injuring this body, walking out of this body is not a simple thing.

Questioner: In other words, they will just sit there and die?

Sadhguru: They don't die; they leave.

Questioner: But the body is left behind?

Sadhguru: Yes.

Questioner: Have you ever seen it happen?

Sadhguru: Yes. We have seen it. We have witnessed with our own eyes an occasion where someone announced that he will be leaving. People have arrived – hundreds of people – to see this. In front of them, the person sat and said, "Okay, I am leaving," and he just left. No poking yourself with a dagger, no eating poison, nothing. Just sitting down, perfectly fine, and leaving.

Just like you take off your clothes and throw them away, in the same manner you shed your body and go. If you understand where you and your body are linked, you can break the link when you wish. Right now, you are talking about stories; you do not know how this life is linked to the body. There is a whole system of yoga as to how you come to this point, where you are linked to the body. If you know this, the point of this coupling, you can release it – gently. Nobody has to forcefully evict you. You are not waiting for eviction. You are a graceful person. When the time is up, you go.

Questioner: Where do you go?

Sadhguru: When you say "where," you are always talking about distances, destinations. Today modern science is proving to you beyond any doubt that there is no such thing as here and there. There is no such thing as now and then. This is just a concoction of your conscious mind. If you transcend the limitations of your conscious mind, everything is here and now. It is not like going from this point to that point. This point is everything. This is not a philosophy; this is physics. Modern physics is talking about this. Quantum physics is saying this. Today even the general theory of relativity is saying this: that everything is just here, one inside the other. There are eleven dimensions packed into the same space. So "where" does not mean somewhere in terms of distance. It is just that you are moving away from gross physical reality. You disappear from physical eyes. That does not mean you have gone anywhere. It is about moving into a different dimension. The same life energy is moving from one dimension to another, from a very gross physical level to a little subtler plane. It is right here, but it is not in its physical form because the physical form naturally went back into the earth.

Now, when somebody dies, you say he is no more. It is not true. He is no more only in your experience. But if you dissolve this information that is packed into this body, if you walk out of your body, then that is the end of the game.

Why would anyone want to end the game? Because they have seen enough. For you, your memory is blocked; for you the memory is only from birth to now. So you think, "Why should I stop the game?" But suppose you realize you have done this a hundred times over; if you saw everything clearly, it would not make any sense to you once again to go through the same nonsense. You would naturally want to see what is next.

When someone leaves his body consciously, he is truly no more. That is referred to as mukti or liberation. The game is up.

APPENDIX 1

ISHA YOGA PROGRAMS

Isha Yoga distills powerful, ancient yogic methods for a modern person, creating peak physical, mental, and emotional well-being. This basis of total well-being accelerates inner growth, allowing each individual to tap the wealth of vibrant life within oneself. Sadhguru's introductory program, Inner Engineering, introduces Shambhavi Mahamudra – a simple but powerful kriya (inner energy process) for deep inner transformation.

The uniqueness of Isha Yoga is that it is offered as a 100% science. It draws on the ancient yogic principle that the body is the temple of the spirit and that good health is fundamental to personal and spiritual development. Scientifically structured, it promotes beneficial changes in one's inner chemistry to accelerate the release of physical, mental and emotional blocks and produce a life-transforming impact of profound experience, clarity and boundless energy.

Isha Yoga involves a combination of carefully selected purificatory and preparatory practices, including a series of dynamic breathing techniques and meditation in simple sitting postures. The practices that are taught do not demand any physical agility or previous experience of yoga. They integrate seamlessly into one's daily life, allowing one to function at optimum level, making peace and joy one's natural way of being.

The programs are designed for a balanced development of an individual, to bring a spiritual dimension into one's perception without disturbing the process of one's life. Thus, ordinary people have the possibility to have powerful spiritual experiences while balancing normal family and social situations.

INTRODUCTORY PROGRAMS

INNER ENGINEERING

Inner Engineering is an intensive seven-day program, where the foundation for exploring higher dimensions of life is established by offering tools that enable one to re-engineer one's self through the inner science of yoga. Once given the tools to rejuvenate themselves, people can optimize all aspects of health, inner growth, and success. For those seeking professional and personal excellence, this program offers keys for meaningful and fulfilling relationships at work, home, community, and most importantly, within one's self. The program also offers the tools necessary to create the balance between the challenges of a hectic career and the inner longing for peace and well-being.

The approach is a modern antidote to stress and presents simple but powerful processes from yogic science to purify the system and increase health and inner well-being. Program components include transmission of the sacred Shambhavi Mahamudra as well as guided meditations. When practiced on a regular basis, these tools have the potential to enhance one's experience of life on many levels.

Inner Engineering is also available online as a practical approach for inner transformation in a fast-paced world. Designed by Sadhguru, the online course allows each individual to experience life on a deeper level with more awareness, energy and productivity. Inner Engineering Online is an ideal opportunity for those with time and travel constraints to experience the same profound effects of Isha programs, which have benefited millions of people over the past three decades.

For more information, please visit: www.innerengineering.com.

ISHA KRIYA

Isha Kriya™ is a simple yet potent practice rooted in the timeless wisdom of the yogic sciences. "Isha" refers to that which is the source of creation; "*kriya*" literally means "internal action." The purpose of Isha Kriya is to help an individual get in touch with the source of his existence, to create life according to his own wish and vision.

Through Isha Kriya, a 12-minute practice, an individual can pursue immediate and ultimate well-being, experiencing success in the social sphere, while nourishing the inner longing for the deeper dimensions of life. Isha Kriya empowers an individual towards a stress-free way of being, and promotes enhanced clarity, heightened energy levels, and a state of peacefulness and joy. Daily practice of Isha Kriya brings health, dynamism and happiness. It is a powerful tool to cope with the hectic pace of modern life.

Isha Kriya requires no special physical agility or previous experience of yoga to practice. It integrates seamlessly into one's daily life, bringing the possibilities of a spiritual process – which were once available only to yogis and ascetics – to every human being in the comfort of their own home. Created by Sadhguru – a realized Master and yogi – it has the potential to transform the life of anyone who is willing to invest just a few minutes a day.

HATA YOGA

Hata Yoga, a two- to three-day residential program at Isha Yoga, is an opportunity to learn *Suryanamaskar* (sun salutation) along with a series of *asanas* (yoga postures). The program does not require any previous experience in yoga or particular physical agility. Participants need not have gone through any previous Isha Yoga programs. In this one-time program, the postures are imparted in such depth and precision that the one who goes through the program is enabled to practice them at home. Isha Hata Yoga is far beyond being a mere physical exercise, simply bending the body. This comprehensive set of asanas is scientifically designed in such a way that through regular practice, one can attain to a certain mastery over the body and the mind. Isha Hata Yoga not only improves health and well-being, it also brings the necessary balance within oneself to experience higher levels of energy. As a preparatory step for other Isha Yoga practices, it significantly enhances the experience of kriyas and meditation.

ISHA YOGA FOR CHILDREN

Isha Yoga for Children offers a unique possibility for every child to experience a joyful blossoming of their natural potential. Isha Yoga celebrates the natural gifts within every child, including their sense of wonder and oneness with life. The program introduces children to yoga through playful and joyful exploration, allowing each child to develop and live in optimal health and inner peace.

Isha Yoga for Children consists of an introduction to simple yoga practices, including *Shakti Chalana* kriya and asanas, as well as the cultivation of a deep sense of responsibility and reverence for life. The program content is presented through fun games and play so that children experience a sense of belonging and unity with life.

Participants of Isha Yoga for Children often experience enhanced concentration and memory, more focus, and improved mind-body coordination. The practices learned are an effective preventative for obesity, asthma, sinusitis, and other chronic ailments.

APPENDIX 2

ISHA FOUNDATION

Isha Foundation, founded by Sadhguru is an entirely volunteer-run, international, non-profit movement dedicated to cultivating human potential. The Foundation is a human service organization that recognizes the possibility of each person to empower another – restoring global community through inspiration and individual transformation.

With over 150 centers worldwide, this non-religious, not-for-profit, public service movement has over two million volunteers worldwide. It addresses all aspects of human well-being. From its powerful yoga programs for inner transformation to its inspiring projects for society and environment, Isha activities are designed to create an inclusive culture that is the basis for global harmony and progress. This approach has gained worldwide recognition and reflects in Isha Foundation's special consultative status with the Economic and Social Council (ECOSOC) of the United Nations.

The Foundation is headquartered at Isha Yoga Center, set in the lush rainforest at the base of the Velliangiri Mountains in southern India, and at the Isha Institute of Inner Sciences on the spectacular Cumberland Plateau in central Tennessee, USA.

www.ishafoundation.org

ISHA YOGA CENTER

Isha Yoga Center, founded under the aegis of Isha Foundation, is located on 150 acres of lush land at the foothills of the Velliangiri Mountains that are part of the Niligiris Biosphere, a reserve forest with abundant wildlife.

Created as a powerful *sthana* (a center for inner growth), this popular destination attracts people from all parts of the world. It is unique in its offering of all aspects of yoga – *gnana* (knowledge), *karma* (action), *kriya* (energy), and *bhakti* (devotion) and revives the *Guru-shishya paramparya* (the traditional method of knowledge transfer from Master to disciple).

Located at the Center are the Dhyanalinga Yogic Temple, Theerthakund, Isha Rejuvenation Center, Isha Home School and Nalanda (a corporate conference center). The center also houses architecturally distinctive meditation halls and program facilities. Spanda Hall (64,000 sq.ft.) is the venue for advanced Isha programs, while the Adiyogi Alayam, a unique 82,000 sq. ft. column-less hall, is an integral part of Sadhguru's vision to offer at least one-drop of spirituality to every individual.

Isha Yoga Center provides a supportive environment for people to shift to healthier lifestyles, improve their relationships, seek a higher level of self-fulfillment, and realize their full potential.

DHYANALINGA YOGIC TEMPLE

The main feature of the Isha Yoga Center, the Dhyanalinga, is a powerful and unique energy form created by Sadhguru from the essence of yogic sciences. Dhyanalinga is the first of its kind to be completed in over 2000 years. The Dhyanalinga Yogic Temple is a meditative space that does not ascribe to any particular faith or belief system nor does it require any ritual, prayer, or worship.

The Dhyanalinga was consecrated by Sadhguru after three years of an intense process of *prana pratishtha*. Housed within an architecturally striking pillar-less dome structure, the Dhyanalinga's energies allow even those unaware of meditation to experience a deep state of meditativeness, revealing the essential nature of life. The Dhyanalinga Yogic Temple draws many thousands of people every week, who converge to experience a deep sense of inner peace.

A special feature of the temple complex is the Theerthakund, a consecrated water body, sunk 30 feet into the earth and energized by a specially consecrated *rasalinga*. A dip in this vibrant pool significantly enhances one's spiritual receptivity and is a good preparation to receive the Grace of the Dhyanalinga. The waters of the Theerthakund also rejuvenate the body, and bring health and well-being.

LINGA BHAIRAVI TEMPLE

Adjacent to the Dhyanalinga, near the Isha Yoga Center, is the Linga Bhairavi Temple. Linga Bhairavi is an exuberant expression of the Divine Feminine – fierce and compassionate at once. Representing the creative and nurturing aspects of the universe, the Devi allows devotees to go through life effortlessly; all physical aspects of their lives – health, success, and prosperity – will find nourishment. The Temple offers a variety of rituals and offerings for one to connect with the Devi's outpouring Grace.

ISHA YOGA PROGRAMS

Gleaned from the core of the ancient yogic science and unveiled for every human being, Isha Yoga programs allow individuals to take tangible steps toward their inner growth. Designed by Sadhguru, the programs provide a rare opportunity for self-discovery under the guidance of a realized yogi. At Isha, yoga is taught in its full depth and dimension and is communicated on an experiential level. The simple yet powerful practices taught in the Isha Yoga programs pave the path for inner exploration and self-transformation.

ISHA OUTREACH

ACTION FOR RURAL REJUVENATION

A long time vision of Sadhguru, Action for Rural Rejuvenation (ARR) is a pioneering social outreach program. This project is a unique, well-defined plan to rejuvenate rural India, the core of India's life-force, to re-vitalize the human spirit and restore the fundamental kinship nature of village society. It aims to create a synthesis of modern and indigenous models of health and prevention through community participatory governance, while offering primary health care services and other services. So far, ARR has helped more than 3 million people in over 4,600 villages, in the southern states of India.

ISHA VIDHYA

Isha Vidhya, an Isha Education Initiative, is committed to raising the level of education and literacy in rural India and to help disadvantaged children realize their full potentials. The project seeks to ensure quality education for children in rural areas in order to create equal opportunities for all to participate in and benefit from India's economic growth.

With English computer-based education complemented by innovative methods for overall development and blossoming of each individual, Isha Vidhya schools empower rural children to meet future challenges. Sadhguru's intention and goal is to start 206 English "computer friendly" matriculation schools within the next five to seven years, at least one in each taluk in Tamil Nadu. Currently seven schools have been established, benefiting over 3000 students.

PROJECT GREENHANDS

An inspiring ecological initiative of Isha Foundation, Project GreenHands (PGH) seeks to prevent and reverse environmental degradation and enable sustainable living. Drawing extensively on people's participation, the project aims to plant 114 million trees and thus create 14 percent additional green cover in the state of Tamil Nadu.

As a first step, a mass tree planting marathon was held on October 17, 2006. It resulted in 852,587 saplings being planted across 27 districts by more than 256,289 volunteers, setting a Guinness World Record. To date, PGH has planted over 12.5 million trees.

ISHA REJUVENATION

Surrounded by thick forests at the tranquil foothills of the Vellingiri Mountains, Isha Rejuvenation helps individuals to experience inner peace and the joy of a healthy body. It offers a unique and powerful combination of programs, scientifically designed by Sadhguru, to bring vibrancy and proper balance to one's life energies. The programs contain a synthesis of allopathic, ayurvedic, and siddha treatments, and complementary therapies, along with the sublime wisdom of various ancient Indian sciences and spirituality. These treatments have had a phenomenal impact on the aging process and have led to miraculous recoveries from seemingly hopeless health situations.

All the proceeds of Isha Rejuvenation contribute toward providing free health care to rural villagers under the Action for Rural Rejuvenation initiative.

ISHA HOME SCHOOL

Isha Home School aims at providing quality education in a challenging and stimulating home-like environment. It is designed specifically for the inner blossoming and the well-rounded development of children.

With its prominent international faculty and Sadhguru's personal involvement in the curriculum, Isha Home School kindles the innate urge within children to learn and know. Focus is given to inculcating life values and living skills while maintaining the rigor of academic excellence as per national and international standards. It does not propagate any particular religion, philosophy, or ideology; rather, it encourages children to seek a deeper experience and inner understanding of the fundamentals of life.

ISHA BUSINESS

Isha Business is a venture that aims to bring a touch of Isha into the homes and environments of the community and to ultimately enrich people's lives. This opportunity is made available through numerous products and services, from architectural designs, construction, interior design, furniture design and manufacturing, landscape design, handicrafts and soft furnishings, to designer outfits from Isha Raiment. All profits from this venture are used to serve the rural people of India through Isha Foundation's Action for Rural Rejuvenation initiative.

HOW TO GET TO ISHA YOGA CENTER

Isha Yoga Center is located 30 km west of Coimbatore, a major industrial city in South India, that is well connected by air, rail and road. All major national airlines operate regular flights into Coimbatore from Chennai, Delhi, Mumbai and Bangalore. Train services are available from all the major cities in India. Regular bus and taxi services are also available from Coimbatore to Isha Yoga Center.

CONTACT US

INDIA
Isha Yoga Center
Velliangiri Foothills, Semmedu (P.O.)
Coimbatore – 641114, India.
Telephone: +91-422-2515345
Email: info@ishafoundation.org

UNITED STATES
Isha Institute of Inner Sciences
951 Isha Lane
McMinnville, TN 37110, USA.
Telephone: +1-931-668-1900
Email: usa@ishafoundation.org

UNITED KINGDOM
Isha Institute of Inner Sciences
PO Box 559
Isleworth TW7 5WR
United Kingdom
Telephone: +44-79 56 99 87 29
Email: uk@ishafoundation.org

AUSTRALIA
Isha Foundation Australia
Suite 1.5, 173 Lennox Street
Richmond VIC 3121, Melbourne
Telephone: +61 433 643 215
Email: australia@ishafoundation.org

SINGAPORE
Isha Singapore,
Block 805
05-636, Chai Chee Road,
Singapore 460805.
Telephone: +65 96660197
Email: singapore@ishafoundation.org

MALAYSIA
Telephone: +60 17-366-5252
Email: malaysia@ishafoundation.org

MIDDLE EAST
Telephone: 961-3-789-046, 961-3-747-178
Email: lebanon@ishafoundation.org

ABOUT THE AUTHOR

Yogi, mystic, visionary and poet, Sadhguru is a spiritual master with a difference. An arresting blend of profundity and pragmatism, his life and work serve as a reminder that yoga is not an esoteric discipline from an outdated past, but a contemporary science, vitally relevant to our times. Probing, passionate and provocative, insightful, logical and unfailingly witty, Sadhguru's talks have earned him the reputation of a speaker and opinion-maker of international renown.

With speaking engagements that take him around the world, he is widely sought after by prestigious global forums to address issues as diverse as human rights, business values, and social, environmental and existential issues. He has been a delegate to the United Nations Millennium World Peace Summit, a member of the World Council of Religious and Spiritual Leaders and Alliance for New Humanity, a special invitee to the Australian Leadership Retreat, Tallberg Forum, Indian Economic Summit 2005-2008, as well as a regular at the World Economic Forum in Davos. He was awarded the Indira Gandhi Paryavaran Puraskar (IGPP) for the year 2008 for Isha Foundation's Project GreenHands' efforts.

With a celebratory engagement with life on all levels, Sadhguru's areas of active involvement encompass fields as diverse as architecture and visual design, poetry and painting, ecology and horticulture, sports and music. He is the author and designer of several unique buildings and consecrated spaces at the Isha Yoga Center, which have wide attention for their combination of intense sacred power with strikingly innovative eco-friendly aesthetics.

Listeners have been ubiquitously impressed by his astute and incisive grasp of current issues and world affairs, as well as his unerringly scientific approach to the question of human well-being. Sadhguru is also the founder of Isha Foundation, a non-profit organization dedicated to the well-being of the individual and the world for the past three decades. Isha Foundation does not promote any particular ideology, religion, or race, but transmits inner sciences of universal appeal.

www.sadhguru.org